מסורה

The ArtScroll Series®

Rabbi Nosson Scherman / Rabbi Meir Zlotowitz
General Editors

A LIFE OF CHESSED

Reb Chaim Gelb:

A LIFE OF

Published by
Mesorah Publications, ltd

CHESSED

*The Williamsburg baker who became
a one-man chessed institution*

by Rabbi David Fisher

FIRST EDITION
First Impression . . . November, 1989

Published and Distributed by
MESORAH PUBLICATIONS, Ltd.
Brooklyn, New York 11232

Distributed in Israel by
MESORAH MAFITZIM / J. GROSSMAN
Rechov Harav Uziel 117
Jerusalem, Israel

Distributed in Europe by
J. LEHMANN HEBREW BOOKSELLERS
20 Cambridge Terrace
Gateshead, Tyne and Wear
England NE8 1RP

Distributed in Australia & New Zealand by
GOLD'S BOOK & GIFT CO.
36 William Street
Balaclava 3183, Vic., Australia

Distributed in South Africa by
KOLLEL BOOKSHOP
22 Muller Street
Yeoville 2198, Johannesburg
South Africa

THE ARTSCROLL SERIES®
REB CHAIM GELB

© Copyright 1989, by MESORAH PUBLICATIONS, Ltd.
4401 Second Avenue / Brooklyn, N.Y. 11232 / (718) 921-9000

ALL RIGHTS RESERVED.

No part of this book may be reproduced
in any form *without* **written** *permission from the copyright holder,
except by a reviewer who wishes to quote brief passages in connection with a review
written for inclusion in magazines or newspapers.*

THE RIGHTS OF THE COPYRIGHT HOLDER WILL BE STRICTLY ENFORCED.

ISBN
0-89906-566-X (hard cover)
0-89906-567-8 (paperback)

Typography by Compuscribe at ArtScroll Studios, Ltd.

Printed in the United States of America by Noble Book Press
Bound by Sefercraft, Quality Bookbinders, Ltd. Brooklyn, N.Y.

~§ Table of Contents

	Introduction	9
Chapter One	Reb Chaim Gelb	19
Chapter Two	Hena Gelb	29
Chapter Three	Reb Chaim's Williamsburg	37
Chapter Four	Reb Chaim's Philosophy of Life	43
Chapter Five	Shemiras Shabbos	47
Chapter Six	Tzedakah	65
Chapter Seven	Chessed	87
Chapter Eight	Supporting Torah	104
Chapter Nine	Children	110
Chapter Ten	Teshuvah and Prayer	119
Chapter Eleven	Midos — Character	127
Chapter Twelve	Reb Chaim's Words of Wisdom	159
Chapter Thirteen	R' Chaim's Final Years	163

∾§ Introduction

WHY IS IT IMPORTANT to write a book about Reb Chaim Gelb? My intention is not to stress his great accomplishments, his myriad deeds of *chessed*, kindness, that he performed during his lifetime. Rather, I am interested in the total man, in the complete person.

What was Reb Chaim Gelb? His intimate friends will first respond, "A *Chassid*." That is true. In fact, he was a Klausenberger *Chassid* and during his last twenty or thirty years he worshiped in their synagogue. But that alone does not make him outstanding — after all, there are thousands of *Chassidim* in this country today. What, then, was his singular achievement that merits being recorded for posterity, so that his exemplary life should serve as a role model for generations to follow?

Let us glance back at the beginning of the twentieth century when Reb Chaim, with his father, Reb Yosef, his mother, Rosa, and the rest of his family landed on the shores of America. What kind of Jewish environment did they encounter? The streets of America were rumored to be *treife*, unkosher. The number of people who were *shomer Shabbos* was infinitesimal. Yeshivos were almost non-existent. The prospect of a young man growing up religious and observant of our faith was bleak.

Generally speaking, in turn-of-the-century America people did not strictly observe the tenets of our faith. The lack of adherence to Torah principles and the emphasis on other concerns led to an environment that frowned on the individual who wished to devote his or her life to following the laws of the Torah. The immigrants' first worries centered on overcoming the language barrier and adapting to the new world around them. Their primary concern was seeking economic security. They wanted to adapt to the American way of life and forget about the mores and customs of their Old World ancestors. Because of this an entire generation was lost to *Yiddishkeit*, although today we are encouraged by the sight of young people returning to the religious observance of their grandparents and great-grandparents.

Against this background we can see how great was Reb Chaim's achievement. Not only was he *shomer Shabbos* and a *Chassid* in spite of the antipathetic, hostile environment of the early twentieth century; not only did he overcome all the obstacles — but he was a *Chassid* of the caliber of the "old school." He attained the spiritual growth of a *Chassid* raised in the rich environment of a European *shtetl*, a *shtetl* steeped in centuries of Torah and *yiras Shamayim*, a community whose members were totally committed to Torah ideals. In such an environment it was easier to produce the burning, soul-thirsty drive to reach great spiritual heights.

Even among such *Chassidim* of Europe, Reb Chaim Gelb would have been outstanding and highly regarded and respected. Yet where was his magnificent character developed? In the arid, barren grounds of America. A miracle indeed!

❈ ❈ ❈

For the reader to be able to truly evaluate and appreciate the events and anecdotes in this book, it would be helpful to understand the social conditions existing during the time involved. For example, in present times poverty-stricken individuals have many avenues of assistance open to them to mitigate their unfortunate circumstances — food stamps, rent subsidies, WIC and Medicaid are but a few forms of government support for the indigent. Social security gives aid to the elderly, the widowed and the disabled. Many other official instruments exist to help the needy and destitute.

Additionally, in the Jewish community there are now many private charitable organizations that provide help in various forms. Generosity is one of the traits of our people. *Tomchei Shabbos* gives Shabbos meals to those who cannot afford to buy them. There are numerous *Bikur Cholim* organizations which do magnificent work providing supplementary health care to those who require it. When tragedy strikes a family, the Jewish public is often called on for help and responds enthusiastically. The Jewish print media is full of appeals for aid for ill and indigent people all over the world.

Free apartments are available in many neighborhoods so that the members of a hospitalized individual's family may be near him to lend moral and spiritual support in his time of great need. People open their homes to strangers so that a family member may be near his loved one on Shabbos.

There are free loan societies now. If a person is in need of a loan for any purpose, these *Gemilas Chessed* groups extend an interest-free loan. There are also currently many institutions in which one may obtain job training and placement. It seems that for every instance in which a person may require aid, an organization of some type now exists to help.

These organizations did not develop overnight but, rather, they are the result of decades of hard work and concentrated efforts by various groups, governments, and individuals. They evolved over time because of the extreme necessity and demands of our people. The development of an affluent society contributed much to the growth of these private charitable groups. Awareness and empathy toward the plight of our fellow Jews were sharpened by events such as the Holocaust. The maturation of the *frum* Jewish community, which now devotes itself to the concerns of our unfortunate brethren, aided a great deal in the blossoming of these helpful societies.

However, in the 1930's, '40's and '50's, the situation was entirely different. Almost all the groups and social-welfare organizations had not yet come into being; those that did exist were not yet large enough to extend all the aid that was required. Remember, the '30's and early '40's were the time of the Great Depression. Adults, heads of families, stood on street corners with boxes of apples or pencils, trying to sell them to the public. A tremendous portion of the populace was unemployed, and for those who were able to find and hold jobs, salaries were very low; the family breadwinner might be earning $15 a week. People were unable to pay their mortgages; foreclosure ensued and their homes were taken away from them. Banks failed and closed down, and many people lost their life's savings.

There was a tremendous vacuum in the area of extending help to the forlorn and helpless. Social Security had just been introduced, and widows' benefits were still unknown. Help for the disabled had not yet been legislated. Food stamps and the like were still many years in the future.

※ ※ ※

The institutions were missing, but the need was there. So Reb Chaim Gelb took it upon himself to become a one-man institution. He raised money to supply weekly stipends to support poor widows and orphans. He helped to put many destitute children through yeshiva, so they would not be deprived of a vital Jewish education. His bakery was always open to those who did not have the resources to purchase food for Shabbos: He gave away *challos* and offered financial help to buy other Shabbos necessities.

Reb Chaim was there to give loans to the needy to help them get started in business. The sick, unemployed and indigent of all types were his clientele. His home was always open to the hungry, homeless and weary. By himself, he filled the void that existed at that time in the field of community aid and social services.

All the anecdotes and tales related in this book are merely a cross-section of the countless ways in which he was able to help the needy. Thousands of Jews were aided by him, and many more were influenced by him in numerous ways.

~§ The Odyssey of Reb Yosef Gelb

For the purposes of this book, the saga of Reb Chaim Gelb's dramatic, creative life begins on the day that his parents, Reb Yosef and Rosa Gelb, embarked on their voyage to America. This journey took place in the year 1901, when Chaim was but a boy of eight.

What motivated Reb Yosef Gelb, the father of Reb Chaim, to arrive at the decision to uproot his family and move them to a strange continent, a new world with an alien culture? Why did he and millions of other Jews leave their homeland, the land of their birth, and move to a new, unfriendly world?

~§ Jewish Life in Europe at the Turn of the Century

Delving into our history we will note that there were several major causes leading up to this phenomenon, social, economic and political in nature. Volumes have been written about these topics; I will merely attempt to give a brief overview. The overall situation in Europe around the turn of the century was so dire that the Jews were literally forced to flee from their lands and their ancestral homes. The economic situation was untenable, the political environment was hostile, there was no peace for the Jews, and the social fabric of these European countries was so interwoven with injustice for the Jews that those who could were forced by desperation to leave. They fled the oppression and hatred that had made their lives miserable for centuries and came to the shores of America, hoping to find a better and freer way of life for themselves and their families.

It is worthwhile for us to spend some time discussing the conditions in the European countries, so that we might have an insight into why Reb Yosef, and others like him, would uproot his family from the security of their home in Poland and move them to a strange new land. The streets of America, he heard, were *treife*, not kosher. He would be confronted there by innumerable obstacles, including the language barrier and cultural differences. But the climate in which Reb Yosef and his ilk lived was not conducive to giving their progeny the kind of life that their parents desired for them. The economic future was bleak; it was a constant struggle merely to stay alive. The political conditions were not bright; wrongs would not be rectified by the governments. The Jew's lot in the "old country" was not enviable — to say the least.

Jews had learned to accept the prevalent anti-Semitism; a cure had not been discovered. However, it was abhorrent and demeaning to them. For example, if a Jew was walking on a narrow sidewalk and a gentile came in his direction, the Jew would automatically move over to make way for him. Similar constant scenes of abasement forced many thousands of Jews to leave their native lands. In retrospect this was fortunate, for had they not left, they and their children would have been consumed by the flames of Auschwitz.

The economic situation in turn-of-the-century Eastern Europe was grim. The Jews lived in countries that were not economically developed and advanced. The populace in general had a very low standard of living, and that of the Jews was even lower. There was little opportunity for employment as there was a great deal of prejudice in the workingplace. Jews tended to be small shopkeepers and tradespeople. At a very early age, Jewish boys and girls were hired out to learn a trade or skill so they could help support the family. Schools and colleges were closed to Jews.

Good nutrition as we know it today was unheard of. A typical meal consisted of bread and onions, with an occasional piece of herring. It has been observed that many boys and girls who arrived from these countries sadly undernourished began to thrive on the American abundance of food, and quickly caught up with their contemporaries.

Living conditions were primitive in the small European towns. Indoor plumbing and running hot water were unheard of. Sanitary conditions were abominable.

Political oppression was widespread. In Russia, the Pales of Settlement had been set up in the nineteenth century, limiting Jews to certain areas where they could reside. The prime locations, of course, were reserved for the gentiles; the Jews were allowed only the less desirable spots. There was no freedom of movement from place to place. Harsh taxes and fines were levied against the Jews.

History records the decree whereby the Russian government could forcibly take young boys from their families and conscript them into the army. They were taken away from their homes at an early age and brought up in the army, in an environment devoid of anything Jewish, in order to estrange them from their people. Many families were destroyed by this decree; no one knows how many Jewish souls were lost in this manner.

Pogroms were rampant in Russia at this time, one of the most violent being that in Kishinev in the 1880's. Without any provocation, and while the government stood by in mute approval, mobs went wild and decimated the ranks of the Jews. The entire Jewish population in Russia was stirred up by these tragic events, and a mass emigration began.

One must realize that political, economic and social factors and conditions are intertwined. For example, if the political system does not allow a person to obtain a proper education, that individual will be deprived economically due to his inability to get a good job. If the social system causes a group to be treated as outcasts, it is needless to say that economic deprivation will follow. If a group is economically poor, then their social prestige will be low, and their political power weak.

One may easily compare our country's system with those in the countries where the Jews resided for centuries. In the United Sates, because of the political freedom we enjoy, many Jews hold positions in government. In every sphere of life we find high-ranking Jews; we are in the forefront socially, economically and politically. In the "old country," on the other hand, the Jew was in a dramatically different position. Very few Jews attained positions of prominence and wealth. As we compare the situation of the Jew here with that of the Jew there and note such a manifest difference, we can easily picture how the Eastern European Jews were motivated to leave their homes for unknown shores. Is it a

Reb Chaim's parents, Reb Yosef and Rosa Gelb

wonder, then, that Reb Yosef left the Old World behind to find an environment that would be free of all the hostility, suffering, and brutal oppression meted out by the other nations of the world?

So, you see, when Reb Yosef made the weighty decision to leave the land of his fathers with his wife and small family, it was not due to an isolated incident but, rather, as the result of centuries of anti-Semitism, lack of economic freedom, and political oppression, all supported and abetted by the various governments of the lands in which the Jews dwelled.

It was not easy for Reb Yosef and his family to forsake their home and the security of the Torah and *Yiddishkeit* that they possessed in their little *shtetl*. They were true observers of Torah, and their lives were lived according to its precepts. The *shtetl* itself, although surrounded by oppression on the outside, was an insular community in which they could easily follow in the footsteps of their forefathers. Giving up their religious security for the *treife* environment of unknown America was not a decision to be made lightly, but required much soul-searching.

✑ Jewish Life in America

America was a barren wasteland, a spiritual desert in the area of *Yiddishkeit*. But this mass emigration by our brethren in the late nineteenth and early twentieth centuries was, as noted earlier, really a blessing in disguise. As we know, *Hashem* prepares the cure before the sickness. By coming to the United States, these early settlers and their descendants were able to escape brutal slaughter by the Nazis half a century later. Once here, they established and built up Jewish communities which have since thrived and blossomed. Large Jewish populations emerged in cities where there previously had been none. We now have in this country many vibrant Jewish communities in which a Torah-true life can be lived — and for this we owe these pioneers our thanks.

CHAPTER ONE
Reb Chaim Gelb

CHAIM GELB WAS BORN IN THE CITY OF GORLICE, in north-eastern Poland. In the eighteenth century, Gorlice had a small Jewish population. However, by the end of the nineteenth century there were about 2,500 Jews there, comprising about half the population of the town.

His Early Years

Reb Chaim's early education was typical of that in any small Jewish community in Poland at that time. He went to *cheder*, studying the subjects that were taught in all religious Jewish schools: *davening*, *Chumash*, *Rashi* and the like. That, we shall see, was the only formal Jewish education he had. Arriving in America in 1901, his family found that there were few opportunities for continuing his Jewish learning. He felt this deprivation throughout his life, and therefore constantly stressed the importance of a Torah education. He loved learning and understood its necessity for the survival of our people.

At the time of his departure from Gorlice, Reb Yosef was already the father of ten children. Altogether, his wife Rosa was to bear fourteen children, ten of whom survived childhood: Moshe, Chaim and his twin Shimon Yiddle, Herschel, Yaakov, Hana, Avraham, Breindel, Ita and Esther. Today the only surviving children are Yaakov, who resides in Miami, Florida, and Esther, who lives in Connecticut.

It is told that before Reb Chaim left with his family for America, his father took him to the Gorlicer *Rebbe* for a blessing. The *Rebbe* blessed him with the *brachah* that he should be a *yerei Shamayim*. Reb Yosef had already noticed in his son, even at that early age, the sterling qualities that would make him such an outstanding individual later in life, and he therefore took only him to the *rebbe* for his special blessing. Because people like him were so rare, his distinctiveness was later attributed to the *Rebbe's* blessing that he grow up to be a *yerei Shamayim*, one possessing fear of G-d.

Details of the Gelbs' journey from Gorlice to the Lower East Side of New York are sketchy. Private cabins for the entire family would have been financially prohibitive, so we may assume that they traveled in steerage, which was the way that most immigrants found their way here. The Gelbs slept in close quarters and shared their small stores of kosher food. It was a stressful journey for the adults but an adventure for the children.

They made their way through Ellis Island without mishap, and found an apartment on the Lower East Side, which at that time was a pulsating, vibrant Jewish community. It is not known where the Gelbs received the money to get themselves started here, as they had no close relatives to give them aid. It is possible that Reb Yosef himself had accumulated the necessary funds to establish himself. His business ventures in Gorlice must have been successful to a certain degree, as they had enabled him to purchase tickets for his entire family for the long sea voyage; perhaps there was enough left over to enable him to get settled here as well.

In those days the East Side — most notably Essex Street — was noted for its rows and rows of pushcarts selling all types of goods and food. This kind of merchandising was popular among immigrants just starting out, because little money was required to become a "tycoon." There was no store-rental fee; space at curbside was free and pushcart rentals were cheap. Some even owned their own carts. Business flourished as people from all over the city flocked to this neighborhood, attracted by the good buys and the variety of products to be found there.

Reb Yosef started a pushcart business selling men's hats and caps. His children helped him in his work. One daughter was

Yosef and Rosa Gelb with their children and grandchildren

*Reb Chaim and his twin brother
on the occasion of their bar mitzvah*

employed to watch the cart and guard it against theft. Reb Chaim was found to have the gift of salesmanship, which he no doubt picked up from his father, who was a clever salesman.

As far as Reb Chaim's American education is concerned, he did attend the local public school for a while, until he went to work in the family business. He learned to speak English perfectly, with no trace of an accent, and was easily taken for a native-born American. A yeshiva education was not possible, because yeshivos were almost nonexistent at that time. Reb Yosef, however, conducted his new home in the same manner as he had done in Gorlice, following the same principles that he had followed there. *Kashrus*, Shabbos and *shul* attendance were scrupulously observed and strictly required of all his children. All aspects of *Yiddishkeit* were adhered to in America, just as they had been in their old home in Gorlice. This provided as good an education for the children as any school could have done.

One must remember that in those days there were many synagogues on the East Side, and the various *shuls* had prominent rabbis as their leaders. It is fair to say that Reb Chaim, although deprived of a more formal education, did absorb a great deal from these religious leaders. He often quoted many of them, citing their opinions on various facets of *Yiddishkeit*. Many *shuls* held regular study groups at which one could procure and absorb a great deal of *Yiddishkeit*; these also had an effect on Reb Chaim's vision and outlook on life and Torah.

Moving on

THE YEARS PASSED, THE FAMILY GREW and then slowly the nest began to empty. Seven of the Gelb children settled in Connecticut, where they prospered and flourished and became pillars of the Orthodox community. Reb Chaim, after meeting and marrying his wife, Hena — whose story is told in chapter two of this book — moved to the Williamsburg section of Brooklyn, where he was to spend the rest of his life.

Reb Yosef was a very colorful and well-respected individual in his own right. When he bought his home in Williamsburg, Yeshiva Torah Vodaath had only recently been organized. Its first home was on Keap Street, in a private home which had been converted to a school. (This has frequently been the practice for many new schools, which modestly begin in a humble abode, due to financial obstacles, and then grow into large institutions.) That is where Reb Yosef went to *daven*. Shiya Wilhelm, a member of the prominent Wilhelm family of Williamsburg, remembers him sitting at the head of the table at *sholosh seudos* singing the Shabbos *zemiros* in that *shul*. Until today, Reb Shiya sings the *nigun* that Reb Yosef sang to the psalm *Mizmor LeDavid* at his own *sholosh seudos* table.

Reb Chaim's travails, and the hardships he encountered in his search for a position which offered economic security and satisfaction while also allowing him to comply with the obligation of keeping the Sabbath, are related elsewhere in this book. He had a great deal of difficulty establishing himself, as did many others who wished to uphold our traditions and laws. Reb Chaim finally found a job as a salesman, and was highly successful in this career.

He remained in this position until the company went out of business. Then came the weighty decision which would change his way of life and, more indirectly, that of countless others. With the full support of his devoted wife, he began to dedicate his time completely to the pursuit of Torah and *mitzvos*.

This way of life is now manifest in Reb Chaim's children, grandchildren, and great-grandchildren. Hena bore Reb Chaim four children: one son and three daughters. Their children and grandchildren now all attend yeshivos and Beth Jacob schools, and are devotedly following the path that Reb Chaim first trod almost ninety years ago.

Reb Chaim and Hena lived at 210 Division Avenue in Williamsburg until the time of Hena's death in 1951, at which time he disposed of his home by selling it to a yeshiva for practically nothing. He lived for several years in a single room on Wilson Street, not far from his old home near Yeshiva Torah Vodaath, where he continued all his former activities, not slowing down a bit although he was becoming advanced in years. He moved from there into an apartment in a new project, where he remained until he was no longer physically able to care for himself.

In the years after World War II, the demographics of Williamsburg changed, reflecting an enormous influx of *Chassidim* to the community. Many old synagogues were taken over by these groups, and they established numerous communal organizations for the welfare and development of the people. Today the community has developed a Jewish character which is a wonder to behold. The sound of thousands of Jewish children fills the byways of the neighborhood. Yeshivos are overflowing with young talented children, which makes the future of our people seem brighter and more secure. It was within this community that Reb Chaim spent his later years. Just as he had been loved and respected by the previous generations of Williamsburg residents, so too was he now loved, revered, cherished and respected. Although it was a different group, they were Reb Chaim's people and he served them with the same zeal that had characterized him all his life. Many groups of *Chassidim* considered him one of their own. He represented the finest in Judaism, and he was at home in Williamsburg.

For the last decades of his life, Reb Chaim was closely associated with the Klausenberger *Rebbe* and his *Chassidim*. He felt a great love and admiration for the *Rebbe*, and although the *Rebbe* was a *gadol baTorah* and Reb Chaim just a simple Jew, the *Rebbe* also manifested love and admiration for Reb Chaim.

When Reb Chaim passed away, his funeral was held at the Klausenberger *shul*.

The Klausenberger Connection

OUT OF THE EMBERS AND ASHES OF THE HOLOCAUST emerged a giant who was to have a great impact upon the Jewish community after World War II. He had experienced all the agonies and torments of the Nazi atrocities, yet he emerged with undiminished greatness to propagate Torah in America and in the Holy Land. Coming to Williamsburg after the extermination of six million members of *klal Yisrael*, his burning spirit touched thousands of Jews and ignited a spark in them to enable them to reach even greater spiritual heights. This figure was the Klausenberger *Rebbe*. After the war he helped the survivors of the death camps and ensured that they remain on the path of Torah rather than fall by the wayside. Upon his arrival in America he embarked on a new project: the rebuilding and creating of a Torah environment in this country. The loss of his wife and twelve children, although causing him immeasurable personal grief, did not dampen his spirit.

He crusaded and preached and established a Torah dynasty both here and in *Eretz Yisrael*. He also remarried and built a new family, imbued with the same principles that he embodied.

He created *Mifal HaShas*, to encourage yeshiva students to complete the Talmud and become masters of it. Another one of his outstanding achievements was the building of Laniado Hospital, which has since become a major medical center in *Eretz Yisrael*.

The above facts alone would have been sufficient reason for Reb Chaim to become one of the disciples of the Klausenberger *Rebbe*, but there was yet another bond. Reb Chaim came from Gorlice, Poland. The *Rebbe* in that town was a descendant of the great Rabbi Chaim Zanzer, and the Klausenberger was also a scion of that dynasty. It was thus only natural that Reb Chaim would gravitate to the Klausenberger *beis midrash* on Lee Avenue to worship with the *Rebbe* and hear his inspiring *divrei Torah*. The *Rebbe* loved every Jew, of course, but he had a special spot for Reb Chaim, which manifested itself in many ways.

Several years ago I was privileged to personally witness the special relationship that these two men had. I was invited to the celebration of an engagement, at which the *Rebbe* was present. He was surrounded by his *Chassidim*, who would not let anyone near him, so as not to tax his failing strength. When I called out to him, "I am Reb Chaim's son-in-law," the *Rebbe* quickly motioned to his *Chassidim* to allow me to approach him. He said to me, "Tell Reb Chaim he should live to greet *Mashiach*." Reb Chaim spent the last twenty years of his life with the Klausenberger, before entering the Aishel Home for the Aged in Williamsburg.

I interviewed several members of the Klausenberger *shul*: Melech Weiss, Mr. and Mrs. Landau, and Mr. Nussenzweig, the *gabbai's* son. They told me that when he was in his mid-eighties, Reb Chaim started to complain that his feet ached. And no

This shtreimel was a gift from the Klausenberger Rebbe

wonder: His schedule at that time ran from 5 A.M. to 11 P.M.; for eighteen hours a day he was always on the go in pursuit of *mitzvos*. I was informed that Reb Chaim had single-handedly closed two stores for Shabbos: Joe's and Shapiro's candy stores. Even in his old age he never rested!

A newcomer came to the Klausenberger *shul* and was perturbed by Reb Chaim's style of *davening*, stating that it was too loud for him. Reb Chaim anticipated his antagonism, and when the congregant turned to face him, Reb Chaim blew him a kiss with his fingers. The man's animosity melted immediately, and was replaced by a new feeling of warmth, reflecting that of the entire congregation. I encountered similar sentiments towards him throughout the entire cross-section of the Jews of this community. The *balabuste* at whose house he ate on Shabbos told of the praise he lavished upon her for her culinary abilities. He used to tell her, "Only a kosher mouth should eat your food," implying that her food was fit for the angels.

As mentioned before, the Klausenbergers told me that he was friendly to everyone, to all races and all people, regardless of status. He always greeted people with warmth and verve. "He was fearless," Melech Weiss told me, and many of the incidents recounted in this book corroborate this. Reb Chaim became the guardian of the Klausenberger *shtiebl*, constantly enforcing the prohibition against talking during the services. Even at an advanced age he stood throughout the entire *davening*. He also took home torn *siddurim* and *Tehillim* books and repaired them himself. He never said a blessing in his house alone if he could recite it before another Jew instead, so that someone else could share in the *mitzvah* by answering "*Amen.*"

Reb Chaim delighted in repeating the words of the Klausenberger *Rebbe* wherever he went. He loved to mention the *Rebbe's* words, "When reciting *Aleinu Leshabeyach*, recite it with the *kop* in the *hoch* (with the head held high)." This meant that although physically one bows one's head when reciting *Aleinu*, one must still "keep one's head high," be full of pride when praising *Hashem*.

CHAPTER TWO
Hena Gelb

JEWS THROUGHOUT HISTORY have always been law-abiding citizens of the countries in which they dwelled. This is due primarily to the tenets of the Jewish religion. Our culture was molded on the precepts of Torah, which demand the highest moral principles from every Jew. The *midos tovos*, good behavior, taught to us by the Torah have become part and parcel of every Jewish soul. Jews are merciful, occupied with doing kindness, and possess the attribute of modesty. Our sages tell us that those individuals who do not possess these traits did not have ancestors at Mount Sinai when the Torah was given; they are that ingrained in our being. So, in all the countries to which Jews emigrated, they were a blessing and greatly enhanced the stature of their adopted lands. In America, too, we have witnessed the tremendous contributions that the Jews have made in every field.

Hena Gelb was the product of such a Torah home and environment; upon her arrival and during her subsequent years in this country she was a productive and valuable citizen. Her beginnings were humble, but her character and upbringing were sterling.

HENA'S FATHER, AVRAHAM MAYER RUCKER, was the proprietor of a small fruit store in the town of Glowgow, Poland. Although he was kept occupied by his business, he managed to spend many hours daily studying Torah and inculcating his progeny with its holy precepts. His wife, Malka, was a true *aishes chayil*, a woman of valor, who helped her husband in his work while raising a family of seven daughters.

Life in the Shtetl

The town in which they resided was one of the small, poor communities which dotted the Polish landscape at the turn of the century. Glowgow had a diminishing Jewish population of about four hundred families, which was steadily declining due to the intolerable economic conditions. Most of the Jews of Glowgow were small shopkeepers who lived in tiny quarters behind their stores and depended on their gentile neighbors to keep them in business. Unfortunately, the general populace at that time was also indigent, and were unable to support the shops at even a subsistence level.

At the end of the nineteenth century, Glowgow did not yet have electricity, indoor plumbing, or any other modern conveniences. Life was poor and difficult.

Schooling at that time consisted of attending the local government schools, where Polish was the spoken language. After school the boys attended *cheder*, where they received a traditional Jewish education in *davening, Chumash, Rashi,* and *Gemara*. Parents who wished to further their children's Jewish education were forced to send their sons to *yeshivos gedolos* in larger towns. Girls did not attend *cheder* — they received the bulk of their religious education at home, although a few classes did exist for them.

There was little opportunity for *parnassah* in Glowgow; financial security was a pipe dream. Poverty was the rule, and Avraham Mayer and Malka found it increasingly difficult to feed their family of nine. It was therefore decided to send Hena to an aunt in America, "to seek her fortune." There would then be one less mouth to feed at home, and her family hoped that Hena would be able to earn enough to send money home to help support her family.

A Young Girl in America

HENA FULFILLED HER PARENTS' HOPES and was able to regularly send money home; it was she who took care of the necessary expenses to marry off her six sisters. The rest of her family remained in Poland, however, and were all wiped out by the Nazis; Hena was the only survivor.

As mentioned at the start of this chapter, Hena was a true product of her Torah-steeped home. She was indeed modest, kind and merciful, and these traits manifested themselves time and time again during her life in America. Her religiosity was of the highest standards. She was always able to withstand the tests and obstacles confronting her, though she was but a young girl of seventeen. The streets of America might have been non-kosher, but Hena always conducted herself in the same manner as she had done in Glowgow.

As was the fate of countless young Jewish women of that day, Hena had to embark on a long, strenuous journey to a new land without friends and with few relatives to greet her. Her possessions consisted of the clothes on her back and her Shabbos outfit. She landed on these shores penniless, but with a home waiting on the Lower East Side, where she lived with her father's sister and brother- in-law.

She got a job sewing in a factory, which at that time was a common position for young Jewish girls. At night she went to school to study English, to facilitate her adaptation to her new country. Thus she occupied herself for the next six years, until her marriage at the age of twenty-three.

The Shidduch

HER *SHIDDUCH*, MARRIAGE, TO REB CHAIM was brought about because of her kind nature and character. The *shadchan* (marriage broker) was none other than Reb Chaim's father, Reb Yosef, who became enamored of the character of this girl.

As you will recall, Reb Yosef had a pushcart on the East Side, near Hena's home, where he sold men's hats and caps. Hena saw Reb Yosef standing by the pushcart all day long, without taking time out to eat. The vendors were afraid to leave their pushcarts for even a minute, fearing that they would lose a valuable sale. Every sale counted when there were ten children to feed!

Eating during the day became a luxury few could afford. Hena was cognizant of this, and brought Reb Yosef coffee and food to assuage his thirst and hunger. He was very impressed by this act of kindness, and his opinion of her grew steadily. He realized that she was an extraordinarily fine girl and would make an excellent match for his son Chaim. Reb Yosef arranged a meeting between his son and Hena and, as Reb Yosef had anticipated, Reb Chaim became attracted to Hena as well. They soon became husband and wife.

True Helpmates

AFTER THEIR MARRIAGE, the Gelbs moved to Williamsburg and set up housekeeping in a small apartment on South 9th Street. They subsequently moved to their home on Division Avenue. Hena gave birth to four children: Avigdor, Shirley, Evelyn and Rose.* She proved to be a skilled housekeeper and an excellent mother. She was prudent with the family accounts, and by diligent saving she was able to accumulate the large sum of $10,000, which was all eventually disbursed to charity.

The home and family prospered, and the house was full of the sounds of laughing, happy, growing children, as well as ubiquitous *orchim*, houseguests, whom they always welcomed.

Reb Chaim was occupied during the early years of his marriage by his job as a salesman, which consumed the greater part of his day, and he was also already engaged in a full program of religious activities. Although he was always busy he never neglected his

---

* Reb Chaim and Hena always called their daughters by their Jewish names: Serel (after Reb Chaim's grandmother, the mother of Reb Yosef, who lived until the age of ninety-five and was said to have known the *Tz'enah Ur'enah* by heart), Chana Chaya (after Reb Chaim's youngest sister Chana, who died in a tragic accident) and Rosa (after Reb Chaim's mother). However, in those days Jewish names were not accepted in the secular world, and the girls were assigned English names ("What's her name?" "Serelah." "Ok — Shirley.") when they entered the public school system. (Girls' yeshivos had not yet been established.)

children in a dignified manner. In addition, she was also able to support one daughter and her husband for two years, while her son-in-law pursued his Torah studies at *kollel*.

HENA WAS ALWAYS SENSITIVE to the needs of others. For example, one of her tenants was a *ben Torah* who lived alone. He was not well, and had no family to look after him. It was feared that on *Rosh Hashanah*, due to the long *davening*, the lack of food would prove harmful to his health. He went to *shul* anyway, however, to fulfill his obligations and do *teshuvah*. To his surprise, before the blowing of the *shofar*, one of the Gelb children brought him a small morsel of food sent by Hena to mitigate his hunger pangs until the completion of the *davening*.

Do unto Others

Another incident deals with an educator in the neighborhood who had to leave for the yeshiva immediately after *davening*, and had no time to stop at home for breakfast. Hena saw to it that he had coffee and cake every day, so that he would be able to do his important job more effectively.

In addition to running her home and business, Hena had the additional obligation of serving Reb Chaim's guests, of which there were always many. She made it a habit to always prepare more food than was necessary for her own immediate family, ensuring that there would always be ample food for the many strangers and guests who crossed her threshold every day. Sometimes on Shabbos, Reb Chaim would march home from *shul* with a virtual army of guests who had nowhere else to go for Shabbos. This often stretched even Hena's resources, but she willingly gave up her own portion to provide for the guests.

Hena was involved with all the various activities of her home, which took up a great deal of her time. However, she was also vitally interested in the human and family concerns of others. Her good heart and innate intelligence enabled her to come to the aid of many families who found themselves in dire circumstances. Her forte was combining *tzedakah* with *shalom bayis*, ensuring peace and tranquility in the home. She realized that people did not merely have financial problems, but often also had human and emotional woes that had to be tended to at the same time.

THIS INSPIRED COUPLE, who dedicated their lives to helping others, was a living lesson to all. People talk of Reb Chaim as a "giant" in his generation, as a *tzaddik*, and it is true that all these accolades are certainly due him. He was remarkable, unique in his generation. But everything that he did was due in no small part to the efforts of his wife, Hena. Reb Chaim recognized this; when Hena passed away in 1951, at the all-too-early age of fifty-five, Reb Chaim took his ledgers, in which were meticulously recorded all the acts of charity he had performed, and tossed them into her grave as she was being laid to rest.

The Ultimate Tribute

Thus Reb Chaim paid an everlasting tribute to his beloved helpmate, Hena, and acknowledged that all his myriad *mitzvos* belonged to her as well. Every good deed was shared by both of them.

CHAPTER THREE
Reb Chaim's Williamsburg

IN ORDER TO BETTER APPRECIATE the anecdotes that follow, let me tell you a little about the Williamsburg of Reb Chaim's day. The Williamsburg of the 1920's, '30's, and '40's was a far cry from the Williamsburg of today. The physical features and the demographic composition of the area have changed dramatically since then. Prior to World War II, the members of the Jewish community in Williamsburg originated in almost every European country; today, the area is populated primarily by Satmar *Chassidim*. There were no housing projects in *frum* Williamsburg then; today there are many, although the residential aura has been maintained in many blocks of the section. Whereas in Reb Chaim's day there was a large population of *Misnagdim* in Williamsburg, today the area is almost exclusively *Chassidish*.

My first recollection of Williamsburg stems from the time when I was a young high-school graduate in Philadelphia who wished to further pursue Torah learning. In the Philadelphia of 1939 there were no institutions of higher Torah learning; the present Philadelphia Yeshiva, headed by Rabbis Svei and Kaminetsky, had not yet been founded. Yeshiva Mishkan Yisrael, headed by Rabbi Menachem Mordechai Frankel, a descendant of the Tumim family, was an after-school yeshiva and not a full-day Torah institution. I turned to Rabbi Leventhal, the head of the Philadelphia Jewish community, for advice as to where I should continue my studies. "Go to Williamsburg," he told me. I first thought of Williamsburg, Virginia, which was so far from having a Torah citadel that I did not comprehend what he was telling me. However, upon further inquiry I learned that the Williamsburg in question was a section of Brooklyn, New York.

Soon I found myself in the Yeshiva Chofetz Chaim on South Ninth Street, which was headed by the late revered scholar Rabbi David Leibowitz, a nephew of the *Chofetz Chaim* and a graduate of the Slobodka *kollel*, which had produced many of the Torah luminaries of our generation.

My first Shabbos in that community was overwhelming. At the conclusion of our Friday-night meal we took a walk down Bedford Avenue. *Shomer Shabbos* people of all ages were strolling down what was commonly referred to as "L'cha Dodi Boulevard," dressed in their finery and greeting friends and strangers alike with a warm *"Gut Shabbos."* It was easy to feel the warmth and spirit of these people.

In Philadelphia a scene such as this would have been no more than an impossible dream. There were few *shomer Shabbos* people in the area, and the feeling they shared was that of isolation.

As the seasons progressed and the weather grew warmer, many Jews would take walks on the Williamsburg Bridge on Friday evenings to enjoy the breezes of the East River. This was another avenue in which to meet and greet fellow Jews enjoying the Shabbos in a relaxed, joyous manner. The late Dr. David Stern, principal of Yeshiva Torah Vodaath, would cross the bridge every Shabbos morning on his way to the Young Israel of the East Side, where he served as rabbi of the congregation. The hordes of Jews emerging en masse from the many *shuls* in the area became another new and welcome sight to a stranger like me.

Later in the year, I observed the whole of Williamsburg converging at the East River to recite the *Tashlich* prayer on *Rosh Hashanah*. It was truly amazing to see literally everyone in the neighborhood meeting simultaneously at the river.

Unlike the Williamsburg of today, there were not many *lulavim* and *esrogim* to be found then during the *Succos* holiday. Many people could not afford to purchase individual *esrogim* and besides, they were hard to come by. We shared *esrogim* with other congregants in the *shul*; few had their own. *Succos* were everywhere, however. These were homemade structures, as the prefabricated *succos* that are popular today were not yet on the market.

Although geographically Williamsburg extended beyond Penn Street, one could say that *frum* Williamsburg encompassed the area from Marcy Avenue and Broadway to Penn Street, though there were some Jews scattered even beyond these boundaries. For example, the Young Israel of Williamsburg was located near Willoughby Street, not far from Gold Manor, a well-known catering establishment first owned by the Goldenberg family and then by the Hirsch family. Rabbi Mandel's Yeshiva of Brooklyn had its roots in that area; this yeshiva counts among its alumni Rabbi Shlomo Riskin, formerly rabbi of the Lincoln Square Synagogue in Manhattan and now rabbi of Efrat, Israel.

The main business thoroughfare was Lee Avenue, which ran into Roebling Street. In the twenties and thirties numerous stores on this street were open on Shabbos; however, with time, Reb Chaim and the Shabbos Council were able to influence many of them to close. There was a *shomer Shabbos* barber shop on Lee Avenue, which was owned by Mr. Welfeld, whose son owned a hardware store. Flaum's was a Williamsburg landmark, where one could obtain delicious herring and other fish. Wilhelm's hardware store was another Williamsburg institution; it was one of the pioneer *shomer Shabbos* stores, and is still run by members of the same family. Kosher butchers abounded, such as Moshe Mintz, Puritz, Lamm's, Avraham Schonbrun, Mendelowitz and Friedman. Flohr's *sefarim* store and printer was then on Division Avenue near the Polisher *shtiebl*. Kaplan's Pharmacy, located at South 9th Street and Bedford Avenue, was the first *shomer Shabbos* pharmacy in the area. Dr. Neuberger was the only *shomer Shabbos* doctor then, and Dr. Levy became the only *shomer Shabbos* dentist, after coming under Reb Chaim's influence.

There were many large synagogues in Williamsburg, headed by prominent *rabbanim* and *lomdim*. It would be impossible to name them all, but I should mention some of the well-known ones. The Clymer Street *shul* was led by Rabbi Kahana, and the Hewes Street *shul* by Rabbi Baskin. Rabbi Melnick was rabbi at the Keap Street *shul*, following Rabbi Simcha Soloveitchik, a descendant of that famous Torah family. The South 5th Street *shul* was led by Rabbi Bunim and Rabbi Pincus, who was also the principal of Yeshiva Torah Vodaath. Rabbi Baumel of the South 2nd Street *shul* was succeeded by Rabbi Teitz.

The Polisher *shtiebl* on Division and Marcy Avenues had a large congregation; its spiritual leader was Rabbi Zalmanowitz, who was also *rosh yeshiva* at Yeshiva University and was instrumental in having Rabbi Joseph B. Soloveitchik deliver a lengthy Talmudic dissertation at the *shtiebl*. The Young Israel of Williamsburg was then led by Rabbi Dr. Sidney Honig. The Mizrachi and Agudah had branches on Bedford Avenue. There were many other private *shuls* and *shtieblach* on the streets of Williamsburg.

Two noted yeshivos were located in Williamsburg then. First was the Yeshiva Chofetz Chaim, founded by Rabbi David Leibowitz, who was succeeded by his son, R' Alter Chanoch Henoch Leibowitz, who has led this yeshiva to great heights and has opened branches in many communities throughout the United States, Israel and Canada. Yeshiva Torah Vodaath had two branches, the elementary school on Wilson Street and the high school on Bedford and Taylor Streets, which later moved to South 3rd Street. The students numbered two thousand strong, the largest Torah complex in the country. There was also a small Beth Jacob school for girls.

The residential area of Williamsburg consisted primarily of two- and three-family houses, with some large apartment buildings. Its inhabitants were of all backgrounds, Jews from all European countries as well as native-born Americans. The Williamsburg residents were mostly engaged in small business: They worked as tailors, carpenters, plumbers and storekeepers, and in many other trades. There were very few professionals at the time, only several doctors, dentists, pharmacists, and accountants.

Today there are countless Orthodox Jews in almost every profession, and large business owners are spearheading every facet of the economy. Forty or more years ago, the businessmen had small factories. They were the "wealthy" members of the community, yet even so they just managed to support their own families.

The more prominent residents of Williamsburg, just to mention a few, included Menashe Stein, who even today is active in Yeshiva Torah Vodaath; the Wilhelms and Kirshenbaums of the Polisher *shtiebl*; the Septimuses, Finermans, Cumskys, Wertenteils, Mendelowitzes, Mintzes, Soloffs, Karps, Belskys, Dershowitzes, Dickers, Gewirtzes, and Ackermans. Other well-known Williamsburg denizens of that day were the Hausmans, Schulders, Dachses, Yarmushes, Honigs, Kogans, Zimmermans, Weissmans, Pruzanskys, Spinners, Piltchiks, Kramers, Fensterheims, Gertzulins, and many more, too numerous to mention.

It is noteworthy to observe that many of the offspring of these people are today *roshei yeshiva*, *rabbanim*, *poskim*, and the like. They, the children and grandchildren of these early Williamsburgers, have branched out into every Orthodox community in New York and to many beyond, making an indelible impression on these communities. It is fair to say that wherever one may travel, one will encounter the offshoots of this venerable community and perceive the tremendous impact it has made on *klal Yisrael*.

Reb Chaim and Hena at daughter's wedding (Jan. 1945) in Gold Manor

CHAPTER FOUR
Reb Chaim's Philosophy of Life

THE SOCIETY IN WHICH WE LIVE TODAY is a very materialistic one, and this has a noticeable impact on the religious community. As Reb Elchanan Wasserman put it, *"Vie es Kristelt zich, Yidelt zich."* Yes, we are greatly influenced by our gentile neighbors' culture. As Reb Yisrael Salanter noted, "If the gentiles knew the effect that the church bells had on us Jews, they would ring them all day." Although we have built many yeshivos and institutions of higher Jewish learning, materialism is rampant in our society.

We have all been in attendance at weddings and *bar-mitzvah* celebrations where the cup of luxury was filled to the brim and running over. Even the *frum* circles have fallen victim to this malady. The vast sums of money expended on these festive occasions could be better utilized to upgrade our yeshivos, which are the lifeblood of our people, and to increase the salaries of the *rebbeim* to enable them to better support their families.

Another area in which this frenzied spending is evident is in the purchase and reconstruction of homes. The prices of homes in *frum* communities have reached astronomical levels. After spending several hundred thousand dollars merely for the title of a decrepit old building, the second stage of spending — that of rebuilding — then begins. Homes are converted to magnificent edifices comprising all the latest architectural and technological developments. Merely walk through a *frum* neighborhood and you will note this ubiquitous phenomenon of beautiful, but shockingly priced, homes.

I was involved in an incident which vividly illustrates this folly. My wife and I took a *glatt-kosher* tour to Canada. While on a guided tour of the provincial capitol in Quebec, the guide pointed out a new chandelier that had recently been installed. He noted this with an obvious feeling of pride and accomplishment. At this moment, one of the members of our tour group made a hushed remark — not intended for the ears of the guide, but only for the fellow members of the group — which broke everyone up. He said, "In _____ (a well-known *frum* neighborhood), they have nicer chandeliers in the bathrooms!" This is an indication of the degree which conspicuous consumption has reached.

On the other hand, the following anecdote will give the reader a simple conception of Reb Chaim's philosophy. It is told that a very wealthy man came to visit the sainted Chofetz Chaim, z"l, in his home. The Chofetz Chaim was known throughout the Jewish world as a great *tzaddik*, a pious man. When the visitor was ushered into the Chofetz Chaim's home he was shocked. He had expected the home of the great world-renowned and respected rabbi to be furnished lavishly, but all that was present in the room were a simple table and chairs. The wealthy individual could not restrain himself and asked, "Rabbi, where is your furniture?"

The Chofetz Chaim replied with a question of his own. "And where, may I ask, is your furniture?"

The man immediately replied, "I am a traveler, and a traveler does not need furniture."

The Chofetz Chaim countered, "I am a traveler too. I am merely traveling through this world for a limited time. We are all but temporary visitors here. We are all travelers!"

Reb Chaim's life was typical of this philosophy. He lived only for *ruchnius*, spiritual values. To him, money had value only as a vehicle for helping others and for performing *mitzvos*. He never desired luxury items, clothing, furniture, and the like. He disbursed to the needy every dollar that came his way. In his later years, when he lived alone, his only furnishings were a table, some chairs, and a dresser. On the wall of his room were signs stressing the greatness of Shabbos and the importance of refraining from *lashon hara*, speaking evil of others. When asked by his children whether he would like them to refurnish his home, he looked at them incredulously and said, "What is lacking here?" He too was a traveler, and along the path of life he wished only to perform what was required of him by the holy Torah.

That was the simple, basic philosophy that embodied Reb Chaim's life: Give, give, and give again. His life was not wasted on the pursuit of material objects, but was devoted to carrying out the Divine injunction of loving and serving *klal Yisrael*.

Those who knew Reb Chaim will tell you that he fulfilled the precept, "Serve G-d with joy." He was always happy and cheerful because his life was fulfilled. He never deviated from the true Torah path, and clung steadfastly to his ideals. His way of life won the respect of the people, although he never did anything for honor or glory, but only for the sake of the *mitzvah* at hand. He never bragged about his good deeds or told people of his myriad accomplishments. These traits of his appealed greatly to all. His virtue was unquestionable, his integrity of the highest caliber.

Wherever one goes, one can still find multitudes of Jews who have heard about him and mention his name with respect. While he was alive, however, recognition was the farthest thing from his mind. All his life he felt that he was merely doing his duty to *Hashem* and to his people.

I met a young married man from Williamsburg, and I asked if he had known Reb Chaim Gelb. He replied warmly, "I always brought my children to see him in the Aishel Home where he spent his last years. I wanted them to see this *tzaddik*." He had definitely made a positive impact on all generations, young and old, during his ninety-one-year journey along the path of life.

Reb Chaim making freilach at his daughter's wedding (right — with top hat) with his late son Avigdor (center)

CHAPTER FIVE
Shemiras Shabbos

"SHA-Boss!"

AS MENTIONED EARLIER, in the first half of this century it was very difficult to obtain work in this country without having to desecrate the Shabbos. More than seventy years ago, when Reb Chaim started out in the business world, the road to employment for Sabbath observers was fraught with obstacles. At that time Reb Chaim had the following experience, during which he coined a well-known expression of his.

※ ※ ※

The stocky young man was running up the stairs with a heavy load of boxes. He reached the top of the stairs and quickly walked over to a table, set the boxes down before a middle-aged man and said, "Here are the shorts and tops that you requested, Mr. Cohen."

"Chaim, that was very fast. I requested this order just a few minutes ago and look how quickly you brought it here. You don't have to run, Chaim!"

"Well, I knew you needed it so I brought it as fast as I could. Get things done quickly and promptly — that's my motto."

"Listen, Chaim, I heard the boss tell someone that he's very satisfied with your work, and that when there's an opening for something better, he'll give it to you!"

At this time Chaim was a young man of about twenty, and was

Chapter Five: Shemiras Shabbos / 47

stock boy and general messenger and helper in Goldstein Brothers' Men's Store on the East Side. He had worked there for several months, and had tried his utmost to please his employers. He was *shomer Shabbos* — he didn't work on the Sabbath. Up to this point no problem had arisen, because he had started work in the summer when the days were long enough to allow him to get home on Fridays in time for Shabbos. Business was slower in the summer, and there was no need to work overtime; although Goldstein Brothers was open on Saturday, they had no need for extra workers on Saturdays during the summer.

Prior to this job, Chaim had not been successful in his quest for a position which could assure him financial security and advancement. In his previous jobs he had worked twice as hard as all the other workers to compensate for the fact that he would not work on Shabbos; however, this was usually not enough to satisfy his bosses, and when faced with the choice of keeping Shabbos or his job, he of course chose his observance of Shabbos over any job. His current position seemed promising. He was trying his hardest to prove himself satisfactory to his bosses, while silently praying that he would not be confronted with the problem of working on Shabbos.

As he was preparing for his lunch break one day, someone called to him, "Chaim, Mr. Goldstein wants to see you in his office!" He immediately set everything aside and went posthaste to his boss's office.

"Come in, Hymie," called his boss, in response to Chaim's knock. "Please sit down. I want to talk to you for a minute. I know it's lunchtime, so I won't hold you long." He turned toward Chaim and looked him straight in the eye. "Hymie," — the boss called him by this name, the English version of Chaim — "I am going to promote you to salesman next week. Mr. Ginsberg is retiring, and I have noticed that you are an industrious, intelligent worker. Are you interested in the job?"

Chaim was astonished. He had not expected such rapid advancement; it had never happened before in all his work experience. For a moment he just sat and stared at Mr. Goldstein.

Then he recovered his composure and said, "Of course I am interested. It will be my pleasure to be your salesman. You can be assured that I will do my very best."

"There will also be a substantial raise for you, of course."

"Thank you, thank you!" exclaimed Chaim. "You will get every dollar's worth!"

Mr. Goldstein dismissed him, saying, "Go enjoy your lunch!"

Chaim was ecstatic; it looked as though his dreams were coming true at last. He couldn't wait for the day to end so he could go home and tell his parents of his good fortune. He rushed home at the end of the workday and, beaming, told his parents of his promotion: he would be a salesman — with a raise in pay — beginning the following week! His parents couldn't believe their ears. Reb Yosef said, "You see, Chaim'l, *Hashem* helps. You have had so much difficulty during the past few years, and now He has rewarded you for your steadfastness in keeping the Shabbos. You'll see — from now on you'll do well."

Chaim was so excited that he could hardly sleep that night. He arose early the next morning and went to *shul* to *daven* and recite *Tehillim*. For the next several weeks he worked harder than ever. He didn't want the boss to find the slightest fault in his work. His sales record became quite impressive. He wouldn't take "no" for an answer, and utilized his powers of persuasion to get customers to place larger orders. When he received his first paycheck, he realized that with his higher salary plus commissions, he had doubled his previous salary! What's more, he was enjoying his job!

Several weeks later Mr. Goldstein passed Chaim in the hall and remarked, "Hymie, you are doing very well; keep it up!" Chaim felt proud and secure: not only had he received a promotion, but now he knew that the boss thought highly of his work in the new position.

One day, a short time after this incident, Chaim was busily engrossed in his work, trying hard to sell to a reluctant customer, when the boss hurried by. As he passed he said, "By the way, Hymie, I want you to come in to work tomorrow; I expect a very busy day." Only then did it dawn on Chaim that it was Friday. He

Chapter Five: Shemiras Shabbos / 49

had been so wrapped up in his work that he had forgotten what day of the week it was.

Stunned, he turned to his boss, but could utter only one word: "Shabbos!" He couldn't think of another answer, and this was the only word that would come out of his mouth. He repeated, "Sha-boss!"

Mr. Goldstein replied, "Look, Hymie, I know that tomorrow is Saturday, but I'm asking you to come in. This is the busy season and we need every extra hand we can get."

Chaim just repeated, "Sha-boss!"

The boss retorted, "Hymie, I know tomorrow is Shabbos. What is it with you? Why are you repeating yourself?"

Chaim said it again: "Sha-boss!"

Mr. Goldstein replied, "Hymie, you must be overtired. You don't understand what I'm saying. Tomorrow you must come in to work; we need your help."

Once again, Chaim said, "Sha-boss!" even more firmly than before. The boss had never had an experience like this in all his years of business. He couldn't solve this enigma. He had made a simple request of one of his best, most devoted workers, and all he could answer was, "Shabbos!" Was he working too hard? Was he going mad?

Suddenly it hit him like a bolt of lightning. When Chaim again repeated the word, the double meaning struck. He was telling him *Sha* — quiet — *boss*! Mr. Goldstein now comprehended the full meaning of Chaim's simple, one-word answer. He was telling his boss to be quiet, because under no circumstances would he work on Shabbos.

He took a long look at Chaim and said, "Go to the office and collect your pay. You can't work here any more." Chaim collected his final paycheck and left the company.

Instead of feeling bitter, Chaim realized that he had passed the test which had been set before him, and was instilled with even greater courage. He dreaded telling his parents what had happened; they had gone through this scenario so many times before, and he had really thought that this job would be different.

But he knew that there had been no alternative, other than to do what he had done.

A short while afterwards Chaim finally found a job with a *shomer Shabbos* company, and was relieved that he would not have to undergo such tests anymore. In the years that followed, he always encouraged other workers faced with the same dilemma. When they were told to work on the Sabbath, he told them to retort in no uncertain terms, "Sha-boss!" Boss, be quiet. This is not your area of power. *Hashem* is our ruler, and we must obey him.

Bringing Shabbos to the Masses

IN THE 1930'S AND 1940'S, the population of Williamsburg, Brooklyn was primarily Jewish, and Williamsburg had become the center of a fine Orthodox Jewish community. Although the Orthodox were only a minority in Williamsburg then, there were already many *shuls* and *shtieblach* there. On Friday nights in pleasant weather, crowds of people would fill the streets to stroll after their Shabbos meals. A stretch of Bedford Avenue became known as *"L'cha Dodi* Boulevard" because of this phenomenon.

Although Williamsburg at that time was the most religious community in New York — and, in fact, in the entire United States — most of the Jews residing there at that time were not *frum*. With this in mind, Reb Chaim wondered how to bring the message of *shemiras Shabbos* to the non-observant majority of Williamsburg's Jews. He then lit upon a plan: Many Jews who lived in Williamsburg worked in Manhattan, and commuted by subway over the Williamsburg Bridge. The subway station at Marcy Avenue and Broadway bustled with hordes of people for several hours every morning and evening. Reb Chaim reasoned: What better platform could one find to disseminate information about *shemiras Shabbos* than on the corner of Marcy Avenue and Broadway, where the trains swallowed up the masses in the morning and disgorged them every night? Where else could one's message be more effective and reach more people?

Thus, every Friday afternoon Reb Chaim took his stand on that very corner to remind the people of the approaching Sabbath. He would recite the time of candle lighting for that evening to the passersby. His purpose was twofold: First, he wanted to impart the necessary information regarding the time of candle lighting. But the second, more important purpose was to inform the people of the approaching Shabbos itself.

Reb Chaim's presence always garnered some kind of reaction. Most people greeted his announcement with a pleasant, "Thank you, Rabbi," as his full beard caused many people to mistake him for a rabbi.

On some occasions, however, people would react with skeptical remarks. This never fazed Reb Chaim; he would always endeavor to answer them properly, as it is written in the Talmud, "Torah is the area where we must answer all questioners."

An individual would retort, "What's wrong with Sunday? I stay home on Sunday and rest. As long as one rests one day a week, what difference does the day make?" Reb Chaim would reply, "In the Torah it states that G-d created the world during the six days of Creation, and He rested on the seventh day. By resting on the Sabbath, and not on Sunday, we testify to the fact that G-d created the world; our Shabbos observance manifests our belief in a Creator. The Torah also states that He sanctified the seventh day, meaning that He made it — Shabbos — a holy day. Sunday is not a holy day. It is a grave error to believe that Shabbos is merely a day of rest, and that any day will do. Shabbos is a day that breeds *kedushah*, holiness. On that day we receive an extra soul — a *neshamah yesairah* — in order to receive the *kedushah* of Shabbos and to elevate ourselves to a higher spiritual plane. We reach these higher spiritual levels on Shabbos because of the sanctity of that day; it cannot be acquired on any other day of the week, even if we rest completely on that day.

"Rest does not mean merely relaxing. We must rest in a way that produces holiness, not by just sitting around listening to the radio. This resting is a sanctified one, and we must keep all the laws of Shabbos to enable us to reach that level. Again, this can be accomplished only on Shabbos, not on any other day. One cannot 'manufacture' *kedushah*; it can be attained only in the manner prescribed by the Torah. Shabbos is one of the ways to reach this *kedushah* because G-d sanctified this day, and we absorb this *kedushah* when we observe the Sabbath according to the Torah laws."

Sometimes, during the course of Reb Chaim's exhorting the populace toward Sabbath observance, people would engage him in conversation and tell him that when they were younger they had kept the Shabbos, but as they got older they grew away from it because of their circumstances in life. Reb Chaim would then ask if they were married and had a family. If the answer was in the affirmative, he would say, "These days, we live in a society rife with problems. Many boys and girls stray from the proper path and cause their parents untold amounts of grief. Did you know that by keeping the Shabbos you can avoid all that?"

Many listeners would perk up their ears at hearing this, as, unfortunately, quite a few families had been affected by this plague. Reb Chaim's solution for such parents is equally applicable today.

"Shabbos is a family-oriented day," Reb Chaim would point out. "On Friday night the whole family comes together at the Shabbos table. Parents and children are dressed in their finest clothes. The food is the best. Everyone joins in the singing of *zemiros*. There is a feeling of family togetherness and purpose. The Shabbos table can thus be utilized by parents as a sounding board to teach morals, ethics, and the proper way to act. How can children learn these principles if not from their parents? The Shabbos table, in its environment of happiness and family togetherness, is the ideal place for these lessons; it is an excellent molding area for character and principle. The background that a child receives in such a home, coupled with a good Jewish education, would provide a staunch bulwark against all evil influences. Try it!" Reb Chaim would plead.

On other occasions, Reb Chaim would be told by a passerby, "What is so important about having a day of rest anyway? I work six days a week, and on Sunday I am very active doing other things. I always like to go places and be busy; I like to be on the go. Who needs rest?"

Reb Chaim would counter with the following argument. "Look," he would say, "G-d doesn't *need* any rest. He is engaged in running the entire universe, yet even He rested on the seventh day, Shabbos. Why? To teach us that every week there is one day on which we, as Jews, must take stock of ourselves. G-d wants us to do this every Shabbos. Activity is fine, but we also must often stop to ask ourselves, *What are we? How should we live our lives? What are our goals?* One day a week, all extraneous activity should cease and we must forget about mundane matters. On Shabbos we take on new activities, new forms of doing things that we didn't do all week. It is a day of unclogging our minds and devoting them to meaningful contemplation and action.

" 'Remember the Sabbath day to keep it holy.' We are a holy people, and this holiness can be attained only by Sabbath observance. Constant activity will not help us reach the end for which G-d has put us on this earth. Keeping the Sabbath will. Shabbos is a time for contemplation and for studying Torah. It is a new way of living, far from the rush and scurrying about of the rest of the week. We must stop! Rest! Study! Contemplate what life is all about — this is our function as Jews. Constant running about aimlessly is not the purpose in life we Jews have to seek."

In this way, Reb Chaim did more than merely inform people of candle-lighting time every Friday. He was a walking forum for enlightenment about the roots of Sabbath observance.

The Making of a Shomer Shabbos

MANY JEWS, UPON THEIR ARRIVAL IN AMERICA from their European communities, found it difficult to establish themselves economically. Most businesses were open on the Sabbath, and the newcomers felt that in order to be competitive and successful, they also had to remain open on that day. Many succumbed to this pressure, and kept their stores and businesses open on Shabbos.

A *shemiras Shabbos* organization was formed to counteract this alarming trend; Reb Chaim Gelb was one of its founding members. The organization obtained a truck, which became known as the "Shabbos truck," which roamed through the Jewish neighborhoods playing *zemiros* and proclaiming the importance of Sabbath observance. Reb Chaim and his friends also took this message to a more direct, personal level, as the following anecdote indicates.

✼ ✼ ✼

In the center of a block stood a small grocery store, with the words "Solomon Silver - Grocery" painted in white letters on the window. The store had been at that location for many years. Its shelves were packed to the rafters with boxes and cans of food; the owner prided himself on his large selection of merchandise. Mr. Silver, the proprietor, stood behind a counter, performing the many duties of the average grocer in the 1930's: finding items for the customers; quoting prices, since goods were not labeled; weighing and measuring produce and bulk items; and, finally, pounding out the prices on his decrepit, old cash register. The store was a small one, but it was always full of customers coming and going.

In the center of the check-out counter was a large ledger. Each regular customer had a page in this book. When the bill was totaled, Mr. Silver would enter the amount in the ledger. Often — as this was during the Depression — the customers would be short of money. Mr. Silver would not let anyone go hungry, and issued credit whenever he could. However, this meant that he frequently had to rack his brains to find a way to meet his own bills and pay his creditors. He had to work long hours to meet his own expenses — from morning to night, seven days a week. Since he could not afford to hire a worker to help him, his wife and children took on whatever jobs they could. It was a poor living, but Mr. Silver managed to keep food on the table.

One day, as he was busy unpacking a shipment that had just arrived, the doorbell tinkled, indicating that a customer had entered the store. He immediately stopped what he was doing and went to the counter to wait on the customer. He took a quick glance and realized that the entrant was not a customer, but a visitor.

"Hello, Reb Chaim," he said.

"Good morning, Reb Shloime," Reb Chaim replied.

The grocer immediately understood why Reb Chaim had come to his store: He had recently begun to badger him to close his store on Shabbos, and had probably come to continue discussing this topic.

Reb Chaim said to him, "Shloime, you work so hard. Whenever I pass your store, no matter what the hour, I see the lights on and you working behind the counter. You know, if you took Shabbos off, you would be doing yourself and your family a big favor. You would be able to spend the day with your family and you all would have a rest. You would really enjoy it — a day of rest and relaxation with your family. Taste the Shabbos, and you will see what pleasure you can derive from it. If you kept the Shabbos, you would see how wonderful it really is."

"Reb Chaim, you are misinformed," Shloime answered. "I want you to know that I came from a strictly *shomer Shabbos* family in Europe. In the old country I went to *shul* every Shabbos; all we did on Shabbos was go to *shul* and learn Torah. I still can taste the *cholent* and all the delicious Shabbos food. The *zemiros* we sang made us feel warm and happy. I loved Shabbos!

"But when I came to this country, I could not find any kind of work in which I could take off on Shabbos. My family pooled their funds to get me started in this little grocery business, and the only way I can exist is to keep it open every day of the week, even on Shabbos. Everyone now is buying on credit, and I can barely pay my own bills. If I had a choice I would not work on Shabbos, but what can I do?"

Reb Chaim replied, "I have been discussing your plight with my friends, and I may have an idea that will help you out, especially since you indicate that you really would like to close for Shabbos. The Shabbos Council has an idea for you. About how much money do you earn on the average Saturday?"

Shloime thought for a while and answered, "I really couldn't tell you; because of the credit situation, it is hard for me to figure out exactly what I earn. But if I could clear about $50, I could survive."

Reb Chaim said to him, "I think we can handle that. I will make a deal with you: Every Friday I will bring you $50, and you will close the store before candle-lighting time and not go anywhere near it on Shabbos. My friends on the Shabbos Council and I will guarantee the money to you for every week that you close on Shabbos. There is one other condition: If you see that after closing your store on Shabbos your business increases to the point that you no longer need our help, please tell us so that we could use this money to help others in the same predicament. Agreed?"

"Fair enough," said Shloime.

The two men shook hands to seal the agreement. Reb Chaim said to Shloime, "Beginning this Friday I will bring you the money. Put a sign in the window telling your customers that you will be closed this Shabbos!"

"All right."

"How will your wife take it?"

"Don't worry, Reb Chaim, she will go along with me. I'm sure she'll agree that we all need this day of rest."

"Okay, Shloime, I'll see you on Friday."

The next day, when Reb Chaim passed by Silver's grocery, he noticed a sign already in the window telling customers that the store would be closed for Shabbos.

That Friday afternoon Reb Chaim came into the store, greeted Shloime Silver, put his hand into his pocket and pulled out a handful of crumpled bills. "Count them, Shloime," he said, as he pressed the money into Mr. Silver's hand.

"Exactly $50," Shloime announced when he had finished counting.

"Let this be a bright start in a new direction for you, which will bring you and your family much joy and fulfillment," said Reb Chaim. "*Hashem* will surely help you and yours for doing such a fine and noble deed. I will come again next Friday. Have a good Shabbos!"

As Reb Chaim left the store, Shloime was overcome with a feeling of elation. It would truly be a blessing to spend Shabbos at home with his family.

Week after week, Reb Chaim stopped by on Friday afternoons to bring him his money and, as promised, Shloime closed the store every Shabbos. They would stop to chat for a few moments every week, and Shloime seemed much more cheerful. One Friday several months later, however, Reb Chaim entered the store to find Shloime with a concerned visage and a look of sadness about him. He looked vexed and troubled. "Is anything bothering you?" Reb Chaim asked.

Shloime replied, "Reb Chaim, please don't think I am an ingrate. I know what I have put you through, and I know how hard it is for you to raise this money every week. But Reb Chaim, since I have closed on Shabbos many of my regular customers have deserted me. When they find that they can't shop here on Shabbos, they go to the store around the corner. Once they start buying there on Shabbos, they get into the habit and start to go there every day. The $50 you gave me covers my losses for Shabbos, but now I'm losing customers and money every day. I think I may have to open again on Shabbos to make up for these losses!"

Reb Chaim was taken aback. He had not expected this turn of events. "Wait a minute, Shloime," he said.

Shloime quickly retorted, "What are you going to do? Give me more money? No, I cannot accept that. I can't place such a burden on you and your friends. It wouldn't be fair!"

Reb Chaim answered quietly, "Don't be hasty, Shloime. You know that every *mitzvah* that one tries to do is fraught with difficulties. Be patient, don't give up so easily. You have made an important decision; don't renege on it. Promise me you'll give it some more time."

"As you wish, Reb Chaim. I'll give it a couple of weeks, but if business doesn't pick up — "

"Bite your tongue, Reb Shloime! Don't even say it. Think

positive! Think that under no circumstances will you open again on Shabbos. *Hashem* will help. If you have true *bitachon*, faith, you will see that you will be successful. *Hashem* will help!"

Shloime was deeply affected by Reb Chaim's words and resolved to emulate his positive attitude. Nevertheless, he found it hard to shake the pervasive mood of sadness that had manifested itself in him. He hoped and prayed that business would improve.

Shabbos passed, and Reb Shloime opened his store early Sunday morning. A few minutes later, a woman he had never seen before entered the store. "Good morning," she said, "my name is Mrs. Goldstein. I live not far from here, and I just heard that you became a *shomer Shabbos*. I try to patronize only *shomer Shabbos* stores, and I would like to give you an order."

Although she had never before set foot in Silver's grocery, Shloime had heard of this Mrs. Goldstein. Everyone in the neighborhood respected and adored her for her legendary acts of charity and good will. Her husband owned a large manufacturing business and, although they were wealthy enough to live anywhere they chose, they would not leave Williamsburg because of its religious character.

When he delivered her order to Mrs. Goldstein, she paid him on the spot. He realized that he had cleared enough money on that one sale to last him for a week!

"By the way," Mrs. Goldstein told him, "my good friend Reb Chaim referred me to you. I am pleased with your service, and you will now have me for a steady customer."

No sooner had Shloime returned to his regular activities in the store when three well-dressed women came in. One said to him, "Mr. Silver, Reb Chaim Gelb has told us all about your *mesiras nefesh* for Shabbos. We and all our friends who are Shabbos observers would like to become your customers." These women also gave him substantial orders, and also paid in cash.

All week long the flow of customers increased, and business improved substantially. Shortly afterwards Shloime Silver was

Chapter Five: Shemiras Shabbos / 59

able to stop taking the subsidy from Reb Chaim, and was even able to contribute a small amount to the *shemiras Shabbos* fund, as his business was prospering as never before.

WHAT MADE REB CHAIM MORE OUTSTANDING than others in the field of Shabbos observance? Weren't all of us concerned with it?

S.O.S. — Save Our Shabbos

In addition to his activities in the communal projects described previously, the following project was his alone.

Reb Chaim had the ingenious idea to appeal to all large Jewish organizations. He sent letters to all the leading Jewish organizations in the United States pleading with them to devote just a small portion of their time to work for *shemiras Shabbos*. He felt that if national bodies would dedicate some of their energy and skill to this cause, they could accomplish far more than any single person could do. He constantly bombarded them with letters requesting them to utilize a fraction of their staff and time to work for this noble cause. He realized that their purposes were important too; he would just ask them for five percent of their time to work for *shemiras Shabbos*. They had the staff, the know-how and the organizational skills to be successful.

Rabbi Bernard Weinberger, Rabbi of the Young Israel of Williamsburg, recalls how Reb Chaim used to entreat him whenever he met him. "Work ninety percent for your Young Israel. Reserve ten percent for working on behalf of Shabbos!"

In his letters, Reb Chaim would appeal to their sense of urgency with the words, "S.O.S — Save Our Shabbos! The ship of *Yiddishkeit* is sinking. Don't overlook it. Do everything in your power. Don't let Shabbos go down!" He expressed himself simply but emphatically to stress his point.

"If there is a flood on the Mississippi River, it affects the entire U.S.," he would write. "If tragedy strikes one section of the country it touches us too, even though we are far away. We Jews are one people. A tragedy in one place affects Jews everywhere. Don't consider it as having no meaning for you if it does not affect you personally. A tragedy for even one Jew is a tragedy for us all. The flood is coming, but we should consider it a warning from *Hashem* to repent."

Reb Chaim's mode of expression showed his depth of feeling, his sincere concern for all *Yiddishkeit*. His clarion call, "S.O.S — Save Our Shabbos!" is as relevant today as it was in years past.

IN ADDITION TO HIS WORK WITH ORGANIZATIONS for *shemiras Shabbos*, Reb Chaim also did his work on a more personal level.

Please Don't Smoke on Shabbos He attempted to influence each individual Jew that he saw to repent and begin to observe the Sabbath.

One Shabbos, on his way to *shul*, he noticed a woman standing in the street smoking. He politely went over to her and asked if she was Jewish. She replied in the affirmative. He then said to her gently, not reproachfully, "Don't you know that today is Shabbos? On Shabbos it is forbidden to smoke." The woman put out her cigarette without hesitation, charmed as she was by Reb Chaim's gentle manner.

So he would do every Shabbos. People were impressed by his approach, which was neither reprimanding nor overbearing, but polite and friendly. When he would ask passersby if they were Jewish, many would answer, "Yes," with pride in their voices. Reb Chaim would appeal to this pride in their Jewishness and ask them to refrain from *chillul Shabbos*, and it was this pride that made many comply with his requests. In this way he taught many uneducated Jews about the sanctity of the Shabbos.

IN THE 1940'S, WILLIAMSBURG was considered the most Orthodox community in New York, and thus the most *frum* area in the

A March for Shabbos with Reb Elchanan Wasserman United States. Boro Park had not yet blossomed into the community it is today; it was a fledgling neighborhood as far as Orthodoxy was concerned. Similarly, other communities that are flourishing today had not yet come into their prime in the 1940's.

Chapter Five: Shemiras Shabbos / 61

However, there is one striking difference between the Williamsburg of yesterday and the thriving Orthodox communities of today. If one walks down the main thoroughfares in Boro Park, for example, on a Shabbos, one will notice that most, if not all, stores are closed for Shabbos. In the old Williamsburg this was not so. The main streets were open for business on Saturday as on any other weekday, as most stores engaged in their regular activities. There were a few *shomer Shabbos* stores, of course, but the majority were not.

It was for this reason that when the great *gaon* and *tzaddik*, Elchanan Wasserman, z"l, came to the United States from Baranovitch, Lithuania, for a visit, and spent some time in Williamsburg, a march promoting the observance of Shabbos was organized.

This march was organized to try to combat the widespread desecration of the Shabbos practiced by many storekeepers in Williamsburg. R' Elchanan was at the head of the procession, and among the marchers was Reb Chaim, who proudly marched along with R' Elchanan.

At this point, permit me to digress for a moment to tell a story that occurred during this period, to illustrate the *derech eretz* and respect that *gedolim* had for each other. One *Yom Tov*, R' Elchanan came to *daven* at the Yeshiva Chofetz Chaim, which was then located on South 9th Street in Williamsburg. R' Dovid Leibowitz, z"l, the founder of the yeshiva, was the *rosh yeshiva* at that time. R' Dovid, being a *kohen*, went up and *duchened* (recited the priestly blessing). After the *davening*, R' Elchanan discussed with R' Dovid the topic of singing during the blessing of the priests. If one were to lengthen the *nigun* (song), this might be considered a *hefsek* (an unallowable interruption in the blessing), R' Elchanan stated. R' Dovid maintained that this was not so.

On the second day of *Yom Tov*, R' Dovid again got up to *duchen*. However, unlike the day before, he shortened his singing during the recitation of the blessing. After the conclusion of the *davening*, his students approached him and inquired why he had sung differently that day than he had the previous day, as he himself had expressed the opinion that it was permissible to lengthen the singing. R' Dovid replied that since R' Elchanan held a differing opinion, he did not want to cause him anxiety or anguish of any type.

Long Live Shabbos

THE FOLLOWING EXPERIENCE was related to me by Mendy Beer, son-in-law of Rabbi Chaim Uri Lipshitz, renowned author and lecturer. Mendy was a student in the Yeshiva Torah Vodaath, and he recalls the experiences that the students had with Reb Chaim Gelb. Making *brachos* with him and answering *"Amen"* were common occurrences to the boys there. However, he also recalls that many times when Reb Chaim came to collect money, the *minyan* was *davening* and had reached the point of reciting *Yishtabach* before beginning the *brachos* that precede the *Shema*. At this point in the *davening* Reb Chaim would call out in a loud voice to remind the supplicants that the letters of the word *"Yishtabach* (ישתבח)," when transposed, spell *"Chai Shabbos"* (חי שבת, long live Shabbos).

And so, like a volcano seething with lava, waiting to erupt, Reb Chaim could not refrain from reminding everyone, "Long live Shabbos!" His emotions and feelings for Torah and *Yiddishkeit* were like a boiling cauldron. His energetic drive erupted from within as he proclaimed, "Long live Shabbos!" He himself lived only for Shabbos.

Challos for Shabbos

REB CHAIM GELB AND HIS WIFE, HENA, drew their *parnassah* (livelihood) from a small commission bakery on Division Avenue in Williamsburg. At that time, in the 1930's and 1940's, there were no *shomer Shabbos* bakeries in Williamsburg which did their own baking; Reb Chaim received his baked goods from kosher bakeries on the Lower East Side of Manhattan.

Times were tight then, and often many people did not have the money to purchase such delicacies as *challah* for Shabbos. Reb

Chapter Five: Shemiras Shabbos / 63

Chaim, naturally, would not allow anyone to go hungry for Shabbos. However, many people felt embarrassed to take charity and would rather "do without." To alleviate their suffering, Reb Chaim set up a system for distributing *challos* before Shabbos.

Many people were in a hurry on *erev Shabbos*, and did not want to wait in line at the bakery. They would submit their orders during the week and pay in advance for them, so when *erev Shabbos* came, they would just walk into the store, pick up their order, and leave. Reb Chaim would prepare packages for his poor customers too. All they had to do was enter the store and pick up the packages with their names on them, making it look as though they had paid for their orders earlier in the week. Thus, even the poorest person was able to salvage his pride and still have fresh *challos* every Shabbos.

CHAPTER SIX
Tzedakah

Reb Chaim's Life of Tzedakah

IN HIS YOUNGER YEARS, Reb Chaim made his living as a men's clothing salesman. He was excellent at his work and made a good living from his commissions. The work was hard, as he had to carry heavy sample cases from place to place. However, he liked his work and did well at it. When the company he worked for went out of business, some of Reb Chaim's colleagues approached him about going into business with them. No investment would be required; his expertise as a salesman was all they needed.

But Reb Chaim made a decision that would chart the way he would lead the rest of his life. He decided to embark on a career devoted solely to *tzedakah* and Torah. Why give *tzedakah* only in isolated instances, he reasoned, when it should be a way of life? At that time, through the prudence of himself and his wife, they had accumulated $10,000 in savings: no small sum for the late '30's. Embarking on his new "career," he disbursed the entire $10,000 during the first year of this new enterprise. It was a tremendous amount of money, yet he unhesitatingly gave it all to those who needed it. This was one of the hallmarks of Reb Chaim's character. He never worried about his personal economic status. He was doing *Hashem's* work; *Hashem* would help him and his family.

He was very successful in his charitable endeavors, as you will see, and amassed a great fortune in *mitzvos* and *maasim tovim* (good deeds).

THERE WAS A FAMILY ON THE LOWER EAST SIDE of Manhattan in dire circumstances, desperately needing help. Reb Chaim, hearing

Empathy for the Indigent

of their plight, approached a wealthy man of his acquaintance and apprised him of the woes that this family was suffering. The man immediately whipped out his checkbook and started writing.

"Wait," said Reb Chaim. "That is not what I want."

"Did you see the amount of this check I am writing?" the man asked, surprised. "If you need more than this, you know where to reach me."

But Reb Chaim again refused to accept it. "Please come with me," he insisted. Finally the wealthy man saw there was no other way, and acquiesced to Reb Chaim's wishes.

The *gvir* (wealthy man) took Reb Chaim to the Lower East Side in his well-appointed new car. When he pulled up in front of the building to which Reb Chaim had directed him, he was astonished. "This is such a run-down, ramshackle building!" he exclaimed. "It isn't fit for human habitation!"

"Come in," said Reb Chaim. "You will see first-hand."

They entered the building and were met by an overwhelming variety of odors. The smell of foreign cooking combined with the stench of garbage in the corridors. The *gvir* turned to Reb Chaim and remarked, "You need a gas mask just to get to this apartment." They walked up several flights of stairs, as there was no elevator in the building.

Reb Chaim stopped in front of a door and knocked gently. The door opened and a young woman came to the door. She recognized Reb Chaim immediately and said to him, "Do come in, Reb Chaim. How are you?" They came in and Reb Chaim introduced his friend to her.

The tiny rooms were sparsely and shabbily furnished. The kitchen appliances were old and battered. "Please sit down," the woman said. The ancient chairs creaked and squeaked when they sat, as if complaining about the stress. Their hostess opened the icebox to get some fruit to serve her guests; when she opened the door, they saw that the icebox was empty except for a half-finished bottle of milk. She turned apologetically to them and said, "You'll have to excuse me — I didn't know you were coming and I haven't had a chance to go shopping yet today." Reb Chaim nodded his head knowingly to his friend, and they realized that the real reason that she had not gone shopping was that she did not have the financial means to do so, and she was embarrassed to admit this.

Reb Chaim's friend whispered to him that he had to use the lavatory. Reb Chaim indicated that it was in the hall, shared by the occupants of the entire floor. "Never mind," said the *gvir*.

Suddenly, four children burst into the room. "Momma," they called, "we're hungry! We haven't had anything to eat today!"

She replied, "Naughty children! Don't you remember, you had breakfast just a short time ago! When these gentlemen leave, I will go down and buy you some goodies. Be quiet now! Don't you see we have company?"

The children, three boys and a girl, ranged in age from two to seven. One had Down's syndrome. All were very thin and pale. "Why isn't your oldest boy in yeshiva today?" Reb Chaim asked.

"He has holes in his shoes and I have to take them to the shoemaker to be repaired. I'll do it right after you leave."

They made some more small talk for a while, and Reb Chaim then asked, "How is Moshe doing in his job?"

"Haven't you heard? He lost his job again and is out today looking for work. Please tell me if you hear of anything!"

"Of course I will."

"Tell me, Reb Chaim, what brings you here today?"

"I was just in the neighborhood and I thought I'd stop by and see how you were doing."

"*Baruch Hashem*, we're all fine, thank you. Everything's O.K. All we need is a job for my husband."

Just then they heard a scream coming from the other room. This was a bedroom, furnished with two rusty beds and a rickety dresser. One of the children had been jumping on a bed, whose sagging mattress had collapsed, spilling the boy onto the floor.

As the young mother rushed to pick up the crying child, the *gvir* quietly said to Reb Chaim, "I've seen enough; let's go. How do people live under such circumstances? Such a young family; it's a pity." He handed Reb Chaim a check for several hundred dollars and said, "I'll see what I can do for them."

As they said their good-byes to the housewife, Reb Chaim surreptitiously slipped the money onto the kitchen table. The wealthy man said to the woman, "Give me your telephone number so I can talk to your husband."

She replied, "We have no phone. You must call my neighbor's number, and she will call us to the phone."

"Never mind," he said. "Here is my business card. Tell your husband to come see me."

As they left the apartment, the *gvir* said to Reb Chaim, "It is incredible! I didn't realize how people live when they hit bottom! Don't worry, Reb Chaim, I'll take good care of this family."

The woman's husband came to see Reb Chaim's friend the next day. The *gvir* got him a good job with a promising future, and helped the family find a nicely furnished apartment. By providing the man with *parnassah*, a livelihood, he helped the family make a complete turnaround for the better.

Sensitivity to the Needy

REB CHAIM, IN HIS LIFE OF *TZEDAKAH*, always made it a point to try and see things from the point of view of the recipient of his charity. One of the things that many people resent is having the borrower of money default on a loan. As the loan comes due, it is distasteful for the lender to repeatedly ask the borrower to repay the loan; on the other hand, when the lender realizes that his chances of being repaid are slim, he becomes filled with bitterness against the poor defaulter. He thinks of what else he could have done with the money, projects which he relinquished to perform an act of kindness, and how he was not being repaid in kind by the borrower who was neglecting his responsibility.

It happened that such a person once borrowed money from Reb Chaim to pay a debt. Time elapsed, but the restitution of the funds was not made to Reb Chaim. Reb Chaim, however, was not the resentful type, nor was he the kind of person who would come personally to badger the borrower to repay the loan. He forgot about the matter entirely and continued to do his deeds of kindness and charity.

Several months later this unfortunate person was again in need of a loan. To whom could he turn? He had already exhausted all possible sources of funds. He had already defaulted on so many debts that he was embarrassed to ask any of his previous benefactors for another loan. Surely they would turn him down this time. His wife suggested that he approach Reb Chaim, but he felt too ashamed to do so. "How can I ask him for money if I haven't repaid him for the first loan yet?" he asked sorrowfully.

His wife replied, "Of all your creditors, Reb Chaim would be the least likely to turn you down." Reluctantly he realized that his wife was right. None of the others would be kind enough to take another chance with him. Even the saintly Reb Chaim would be completely within his rights to turn him down, he thought, but he had no one else to turn to.

With trepidation he set out for Reb Chaim's house. He arrived at the Gelb home, where Hena invited him in graciously and went to inform her husband about their visitor. Reb Chaim understood right away what the purpose of this visit was. He greeted his visitor and, without giving him a chance to speak, said, "Perhaps you could help me out. I find myself with some extra money left over, and I was thinking, maybe you could use it. I have no need for it now and I don't like to leave unused money lying around. Please take it, and pay me back whenever you get the chance."

The man was shocked at Reb Chaim's faith in him. He took the money, thanked Reb Chaim profusely, and left.

The Talmud states in Tractate *Bava Basra*, "He who gives charity to a poor man receives six blessings. However, he who consoles him is blessed with eleven blessings." Reb Chaim realized how important it is to ease the troubled mind of the needy. He understood that the hand extended to him for help was not comfortable or at ease with the situation — no one likes to request aid. Reb Chaim always took this into consideration in his deeds of charity, and was careful to first and foremost set the minds of the needy at ease.

HESHY MILLET, A PROMINENT MEMBER of the catering establishment, recalls with sentiment the occasions that he gave Reb Chaim charity for his various causes. He always gave Reb Chaim the same sum of money and was always thanked graciously.

A Feeling of Sensitivity

After his marriage to Henrietta Askowitz, Heshy bumped into Reb Chaim and received a hearty *"Mazel Tov!"* He proffered his usual offering to Reb Chaim, but before it was accepted, Reb Chaim asked him, "Now that you are married, do you think you can afford this?"

Reb Chaim was sensitive to the giver's financial conditions, as well as to the conditions of his many recipients. Heshy assured him that he could still afford to give him this amount. It was only then that Reb Chaim accepted the money.

Others have related similar incidents. One young gentleman, in a moment of inspiration, offered Reb Chaim a sizable sum. Reb Chaim handed it back to him, saying, "You cannot afford this."

Mrs. Gewirtz told me that Reb Chaim would never take money from her twice in a single day. "You gave to me already," he would tell her. Reb Chaim was indeed sensitive to all people, not only to the needy.

IT WAS A WARM DAY IN SUMMER. It had been a rainy summer that year, and it looked that day as though the pattern would continue. The sky was threatening, filled with ominous-looking clouds. People were scurrying for shelter, afraid of the oncoming storm. No one ventured outside without a raincoat and rubbers.

The Coat off His Back

Reb Chaim was just finishing breakfast and was getting ready to make his scheduled neighborhood rounds. As he started for the front door, Hena called to him, "Chaim, don't forget to take your raincoat and rubbers, it looks like rain again."

Reb Chaim had no time to argue. He went to the closet and began to rummage inside for his overshoes. After several moments of futile searching, he emerged defeated. "It can't be possible," he said. "I remember putting my rubbers in the closet and now they're just not here!"

"You've forgotten," Hena sighed. "The last time it rained you gave away your rubbers in *shul* to someone who had forgotten to wear his. You're always doing that. I think I have bought more rubbers than any other woman in New York! To tell you the truth, I bought you yet another pair; they're still in the box in my closet. But please, I want you to promise not to give this pair away. I know you mean well, but when you need them you haven't any either!" She went to her closet and found the new pair of rubbers for her husband.

Reb Chaim thought to himself, "She is right, but what else can I do when I see a person in *shul* who has a long walk home in this bad weather? A man could get sick walking such a long way in the rain. His feet could get wet, and he will catch cold. Somehow, I never do catch colds, so it's better for him to have my rubbers. What can I do?"

He took the proffered rubbers and slipped them over his shoes. He put on his raincoat and went out the door with his usual parting remark. "I don't know exactly when I'll be home," he said, "so don't worry if I'm late."

He was humming as he left home; starting off on a day of charity and good deeds always put him in a fine mood. As he looked up at the sky, he noted that Hena had been right again; it would probably rain very soon. He began to make his rounds. First he attended a meeting of the Shabbos Council to discuss methods of convincing storekeepers to close for Shabbos. Next he paid a visit to a recently widowed woman who had been left with three young children. He greeted her and inquired if everything was all right with them. He handed her an envelope, stating, "I found this in your mailbox." He had followed this procedure for several months and continued to do so until she was able to support herself again.

His next stop was to visit Reb Mottel. Reb Mottel was a Torah scholar who was severely handicapped. His family lived far away and he had no one to help him in his daily activities. He looked forward to Reb Chaim's weekly visits, as they would have a chance to discuss Torah while Reb Chaim helped him out. Reb Chaim brought him groceries, and helped Reb Mottel to bathe; he then prepared a meal for him. By the time Reb Chaim was ready to leave, the rainstorm had begun and he was glad that he had taken his raincoat and rubbers.

As he walked to his next stop in the downpour, he noticed someone approaching him. It was an old bearded Jew, walking in the rain without a raincoat. Reb Chaim stopped him and asked, "Where is your raincoat in this weather?"

The man replied in Yiddish, *"Ich hab nisht kein regenmantle* (I have no raincoat)." Reb Chaim said to him, also in Yiddish, *"Ihr vet veren krank!* (You will become ill)!" Before the man could react, Reb Chaim slipped off his raincoat and quickly put it on him. Over the other man's strong objections, Reb Chaim also gave him his rubbers. Reb Chaim was then off and running, and gave the man no chance to return the items. Taken off guard, the man had no choice but to keep the raincoat and rubbers.

Reb Chaim returned home soaked to the skin. A puddle formed around his feet where he stood. Hena saw him and shrieked, "Chaim, what happened to you? Were you robbed? Where are your raincoat and rubbers?" Her words were pouring as fast as the rain.

Reb Chaim calmly reassured her. "No, nothing like that happened. I met someone who needed them more than I did. If you would have seen that poor, old, soaking-wet Jew, you would have done the same."

"And what about this poor soaking-wet Jew?" She pointed at her husband. "Who is going to take care of him?"

Reb Chaim quickly changed to dry clothes so he could continue his rounds, for there were many people who depended on him. But Hena refused to let him out the door. "No, you don't!" she called. "Get back in here! You're not going out without a raincoat."

"But how can I let these people down? They're counting on me."

"Wait here," Hena said, and ran out. She went to a neighbor's home and was able to procure an extra raincoat and rubbers for him. "Here, now you can continue your work. You know I'm glad to be part of this *mitzvah*."

The Bekeshe that Never Was

REB CHAIM DESIRED NO WORLDLY GOODS for himself and, indeed, he possessed very few. He had priorities — for him it was more important to alleviate the sufferings and hardships of others than to enjoy a material object himself. As you just read, he would literally give the coat off his back to the needy.

When the first of his grandchildren became engaged to be married and all the arrangements for the wedding had been completed, Reb Chaim's family gave him money to purchase a new *bekeshe* (frock coat) for this great *simchah*. "You are a member of the *chassan's* family," they told him. "You should appear in nice new clothing, as befits the occasion." He acquiesced and assured everyone that he would be there with the proper attire.

On the night of the wedding, everyone was assembled at the hall and enjoying themselves when Reb Chaim made his appearance. He immediately disappeared into the throngs of people enjoying the *simchah*. We, the family, didn't catch sight of him for quite a while, as he was busy receiving *Mazel Tov* wishes from all his acquaintances. Finally he approached the family circle and noted a collective look of disappointment shadowing our faces. He nodded knowingly, shrugged his shoulders and said to us, "Some poor Jew needed a new coat much more than I did, so I gave him the *bekeshe* money. What else could I do?"

WHEN REB CHAIM MARRIED OFF his daughter Rose, the wedding was held at the Clymer Street *shul* in Williamsburg. As I mention elsewhere in this book, Reb Chaim's home was an open house for poor people who knew they could receive food and lodging there whenever they needed it. Over the years many of these people had become like members of the family; they were always about, and everyone engaged them in conversation like other friends and relatives. No one would even think that they were poor people waiting for a meal. Reb Chaim, his wife and children treated them like any other good friends of the family.

The Poor Sit at the Head of the Table

So it came to pass that when Reb Chaim's daughter Rose married Phil Rosenberg, he invited all these people to the wedding. When the seating arrangements were made, however, he did not put them with the other guests, to whom they were strangers and with whom they might feel uncomfortable. Instead, he placed them at the head table with the bride and groom and other members of the family, with whom they would feel at home. Thus they were able to participate and enjoy themselves like any other guests.

To Reb Chaim there was no line between Jew and Jew. Rich or poor, we are all brothers.

HERSH LEIB WAS A MAN IN HIS MID-FORTIES. He was a rather nondescript individual save for his eyes, which protruded from their sockets as if he were seeking something. His skin was pale and sallow as a result of years of incarceration in a concentration camp. He had a thick, wild, uncultivated black moustache below a small, chiseled nose. But it was his eyes that left an impression on the beholder. There was an aura of sadness about him, emanating from the inner emotions and feelings which he had experienced during the Holocaust.

The Highest Form of Charity

Hersh Leib's entire family — his wife, two sons, and two daughters, and more than sixty relatives — had been taken from him and exterminated in the Nazi death camps. He was the only survivor. His entire reason for living had been extirpated. It was no wonder, then, that Hersh Leib had such a sad mien. He had despaired of ever again finding happiness or contentment.

However, life does go on, and after the war he met a young woman who had also managed to survive the atrocities. They married and had two children. But Hersh Leib felt that he could no longer live in Germany. The blood of his brethren was still crying to him from the earth. It was not possible for him to continue to exist on this blood-drenched soil. He was constantly haunted by his memories, and wanted to come to the United States to make a fresh start. He communicated with an uncle he had in this country, pleading with him to get visas for him and his family. After an agonizing wait he received the necessary papers and tickets to come to America.

His joy was unbounded — at last there was hope for a new life for him and his new family. He was still young — he could go to America and build a little home, helping in a minuscule way to rebuild the *churban*, the destruction of his people.

In Europe, Hersh Leib had always been a scrupulous observer of all the Orthodox traditions of the generations before him. During the war, even in the face of death, he refused to give up his observance of the laws of the Torah. His new wife was of the same school, and they had begun to build a true Torah home. However, his American uncle did not share his views. Though he accommodated Hersh Leib and his family by supplying them with kosher food in his nonobservant home, Hersh Leib — although everlastingly grateful for all his uncle had done for him — realized that his stay at his uncle's home must be a short one. He broached the subject to his uncle of finding his own apartment in a neighborhood where there were Orthodox Jews. His uncle said that he would see what could be done.

Several weeks later his uncle said to him, "Hersh Leib, I have good news for you. A friend of mine has an apartment building in Williamsburg and he will let you have an apartment at no charge until you are able to get yourself started."

Hersh Leib's first question was, "Is Williamsburg like your community here on Long Island, or is it a more religious area?"

His uncle replied, "You may not have heard of it, but Williamsburg is the most religious area in New York."

"Great! When will I be able to move in?"

"I will try to get you some furniture, and then you can move in immediately."

This took several more weeks; Hersh Leib could hardly wait. Finally everything was set up. Hersh Leib expressed his thanks to his uncle, and they set off for Williamsburg in his uncle's car.

Hersh Leib was a bit taken aback at the sight of his new apartment. It was a run-down apartment in a run-down building in a run-down section of Williamsburg. He concealed his disappointment because he didn't want to appear ungrateful to his uncle, who had done so much for him. He kissed his uncle and thanked him profusely for everything he had done. His uncle sat him down at the table and told him, "Don't be disappointed by this apartment. Remember, it is only temporary until you can get yourself a job." As he left, he handed Hersh Leib an envelope. Hersh Leib opened it and found that it contained $50; he would have to use it sparingly until he found the means to support himself and his family.

The next day he set out early to find a *shul*. To his great anguish, he found that all the people he approached on the street were not Jewish, nor did they know of a synagogue in that neighborhood. He was amazed. Where were the Jews? Wasn't this Williamsburg, the most religious neighborhood in New York? At last he spotted a kosher butcher shop and went inside to ask the butcher for directions to the nearest *shul*. It turned out to be about eight blocks from his home, and he arrived just in time for services. After *davening* he became acquainted with the worshipers and, to his chagrin, found out that the part of Williamsburg in which his apartment was located was not the *frum* section at all. This was an additional impetus for him to get out right away and begin his search for employment, as the sooner he got back on his feet the sooner he would be able to move to a proper home.

Early every morning he set out looking for jobs or businesses, anything worthwhile that would help him maintain his family. The days and weeks went by, but he still had not found anything. He was already exhausting his meager funds. Finally, out of desperation, he decided to go down to the *frum* area of Williamsburg; maybe he would find a *landsman* (European neighbor) or family who could help him get started. His own neighborhood was populated by small tradesmen and workers who were also struggling to make ends meet; he could find no succor there. So he took a bus to Yeshiva Torah Vodaath, as he had heard in his daily wanderings that this place was a center of Torah, and many *frum* Jews came there to pray and learn.

His mood and spirit were elevated as soon as he entered the building. He felt grand — these were the people he wanted to live with and get to know. He put on his *tallis* and *tefillin* to *daven*, and felt that after services he would be able to speak to someone to make them aware of his family's plight. Perhaps he would be able to find a lead to help him get started.

After the prayers were over, the congregants left one by one for their jobs and businesses. The realization struck Hersh Leib that these people were all busy and would have no time for him! Everyone was on his way out, and soon he would be left alone again. Suddenly, all the emotion and pent-up feelings that he had kept stored inside for years burst out like a waterfall. This was his last hope, and now it too was dashed. The tears cascaded from his eyes. He stood in his place, crying quietly, as he did not want anyone to notice his grief.

One sharp and sensitive congregant did notice, however, and was affected by the tears of Hersh Leib. It was, of course, Reb Chaim Gelb. After World War II thousands of displaced Jews had made their way to the shores of America and struggled to establish themselves financially. They had no means of support and no families to help them. Reb Chaim had reached out to many; he had met them, spoken to them and aided them. So when he beheld this despondent, tearful Jew, crying with such heartbreak, he empathized with him. He could spot the pride in this person who was trying to cry silently. Not wishing to intrude upon his personal emotions, Reb Chaim handed some money to his son and nodded towards the crying man. Without another word, his son approached the sobbing man, gave him the money and walked away.

This unexpected act of kindness was a turning point for Hersh Leib. He felt that there indeed were sympathetic people in America! He stopped crying and began to think of how he could best invest this windfall. He hit upon the idea of buying some costume jewelry — he had been a jeweler in Europe — and endeavoring to sell it. He did so and turned a handsome profit, which he used to expand his business. Day by day he followed this procedure and became a successful businessman. In the years that followed he never forgot Reb Chaim and his generosity in his hour of greatest need.

Rambam (Maimonides) lists the eight levels of giving charity. He states that enabling someone to earn his own *parnassah* — what Reb Chaim was able to do in this case — is the highest form of charity.

Supporting an Entire Village

AS I RESEARCHED THIS BOOK, I WAS AMAZED by the discovery of astounding facts that hitherto were unknown to me and to my family. Mr. and Mrs. Bernard Gewirtz, daughter and son-in-law of the late Reb Binyomin Wilhelm, one of the founders of Yeshiva Torah Vodaath, related this tale to me.

The in-laws of the late Nat Saperstein, former president of the National Council of Young Israel, had a small grocery store in Williamsburg that was patronized by the Gewirtzes. Once, while they were shopping in the store, the proprietor related to them that he had been to *Eretz Yisrael*, and had visited a small town there. When he and his wife mentioned to the village's inhabitants that they were from Brooklyn, they were besieged by queries as to whether they knew Chaim Gelb. Their curiosity was aroused by this constant questioning. When they asked the people how they knew the name of Chaim Gelb, they were told that Reb Chaim supported the entire village almost single-handedly.

Although this may seem incredible to those who did not know him, this fits the pattern of his deeds and was well within the realm of his activities. The Israeli villagers all knew him and praised him highly, but since Reb Chaim never searched for glory for his deeds, this mammoth undertaking of supporting an entire Israeli village was virtually unknown to the American community.

Reb Chaim and the Beth Jacob Seminary

THE BETH JACOB SEMINARY OF WILLIAMSBURG was the first of its kind in America. For many years it was located on South 8th Street near Bedford Avenue. It was run by R' Baruch Kaplan, former *Rosh Yeshiva* of Torah Vodaath, and his *rebbetzin*, z"l. Girls came from all over America to study there. Many illustrious *rebbetzens*, educators and other learned women who have since distinguished themselves were educated in that school. They benefited from the *mesiras nefesh* of the leaders of Beth Jacob who, because of the precarious financial situation of those days, had to work tirelessly just to keep the institution running.

From the time yeshivos were started in this country up to the present day, one tool frequently utilized to ease the financial burdens of operating was taking out loans. If a yeshiva or seminary had no money, borrowing was sometimes the only solution, at least for a while, to ease the burden. When the Beth Jacob Seminary needed funds, Rabbi Kaplan turned to Reb Chaim Gelb, who went to various *gemilas chessed* societies to obtain the loans.

Reb Chaim was thus instrumental in getting the loans which were so vital to Beth Jacob's existence and survival. Financial conditions being what they were at that time, it was difficult even to meet the payments on these loans. They were given only for a specific period, and they had to be paid on time. Reb Chaim was completely aware of the situation of Beth Jacob, and before Rabbi Kaplan would approach him to tell him that he could not meet the loan payments in a given month, Reb Chaim would have taken care of the loans on his own. He made the rounds to all the loan

Chapter Six: Tzedakah / 79

societies and renewed them for another six months or a year. He informed Rabbi Kaplan of his efforts after his goals had been accomplished, and helped set Rabbi Kaplan's mind at ease so he could concentrate on the holy task of educating the daughters of Israel. Reb Chaim had a great deal to do with the successful development of these scholarly and religious Jewish women. This Beth Jacob Seminary was the forerunner of the present seminary in Boro Park, where Rabbi Kaplan is still at the helm today.

Collecting Money at Weddings

EVERYONE WHO HAS ATTENDED A *FRUM* WEDDING can attest to this phenomenon: Before the ceremony, while the guests are socializing and participating in the consumption of a smorgasbord, they are besieged by hordes of collectors for various causes. One person is collecting for *hachnasas kallah*, another for the sick, and so on. As we all know, there is never a lack of indigent people or worthy causes. And the Jewish heart is always open, especially during a *simchah* such as a wedding; when one is happy and joyful, one responds to others' pleas more readily. My son-in-law, Shaya Schonbrun, relates that when his sister Sury married Sammy Bialik in a plush hotel, he and his father, Irving Schonbrun, discussed the above situation. They decided to give each collector a significant sum on the promise that they would refrain from further collecting. This would result in a nicer, more orderly affair. Shaya tells me that his father then told him that they would allow only one exception to their rule: The "little man," Reb Chaim Gelb, could collect as usual. Little did Shaya realize at that time that Reb Chaim would eventually become his grandfather, when Shaya married Reb Chaim's granddaughter Malka!

This occurrence was not a singular or unique one. There were many occasions when people who wished to avoid the excessive soliciting of charity at their children's weddings would give a sizable stipend to each collector on the condition that they do no further collecting. But frequently they made exceptions for Reb

Chaim, since he was so beloved by them all. His smiling countenance and abundance of good cheer added a special touch to every wedding. His devotion and sincerity were widely known, and people felt honored by his presence at their *simchos*.

Many times I have met people who informed me with pride that they gave Reb Chaim money for charity. They always felt it an honor to be able to participate in his causes.

Reb Chaim's Ledger

THE TALMUD, IN TRACTATE *BAVA BASRA* 8b, says about the distributors of charity, "Those who make the public righteous will shine like stars forever." By collecting the dollars of friends and neighbors, combining them to make large sums, collectors and distributors of charity attribute many fine and righteous deeds to the public, deeds which as individuals few could accomplish. No one person can by himself answer the calls of all the needy; however, by contributing as much as he can, he adds to a cumulative amount which can reach awesome proportions.

One could take a look into Reb Chaim's ledger and see the words of our Sages manifested between the lines. The pennies, dimes, and dollar bills that made their way into Reb Chaim's hands were no longer minuscule, insignificant amounts that had no value; they miraculously became large sums capable of aiding the sick and the poor. Each individual donation had but a tiny impact; taken collectively, they were a great source of help and succor to the needy.

Reb Chaim kept a different page for each month. His ledger sheet would look something like this:

Collections
Month of Cheshvan

1 Cheshvan
$26.00

2 Cheshvan
$58.00

3 Cheshvan
$47.00

and so on. He would carefully add up the total for every month.

The corresponding page would run as follows:

Disbursements
Month of Cheshvan

1 Cheshvan
$20.00 — *Talmid chacham*
$15.00 — Tuition for poor children
$36.00 — Widow with sick children

2 Cheshvan
$50.00 — Newly arrived immigrant
$20.00 — Yeshiva

3 Cheshvan
$20.00 — Doctor for sick person
$25.00 — Unemployed father of three

He never mentioned the names of anyone who received his charity, so as not to embarrass the recipients. However, he knew them all and never forgot who was in need.

A pattern is easily apparent here: He disbursed more money than he collected. The difference was usually made up from his own pocket.

The ledger served a purpose other than being a record of collections and disbursements. It also served to keep track of the needy and ensure that those who required assistance were getting what they needed. These payments were not one-time gifts, but part of a long-term project aimed at trying to solve the indigent's problem and helping that person to get back on his or her own feet. He helped sustain the needy person for as long as it took, whether months or even years.

He put a description of each person in the ledger so no one would be forgotten. To the outsider, the entries seemed to be no more than numbers and incomprehensible scrawls, but to Reb Chaim each mark represented an individual whom he knew personally. The book brought tears to his eyes as he recalled the suffering of those who were entered in it; it had great symbolic value to him. To some people, a bankbook is the most important book in their lives; to Reb Chaim, this book meant more than money in the bank — it meant helping others and easing their lives. In and through it he relived the many heroic struggles of people trying to overcome overwhelming odds, and he felt proud to have been a contributor to their eventual success.

In a conversation I had with Rabbi Yisrael Belsky, prominent *rosh yeshiva* in Torah Vodaath and a grandson of Reb Binyamin Wilhelm, he revealed to me that he had seen Reb Chaim's ledger when he was a youth. (No one I know had really gone through it page by page.) He had seen large sums listed, such as $5,000 donated to Beth Jacob or $10,000 to Torah Vodaath. Rabbi Belsky was amazed at the size of the figures, which were even more enormous by the standards of that time. Few people knew of the great breadth and scope of the sums that Reb Chaim distributed to charity over his lifetime.

The ledger was an integral portion of his life. His charitable undertakings were inscribed in it as our good deeds are inscribed in the Book of Life. His life's work, his goals, his *maasim tovim* were all inscribed there. It was, in essence, a microcosm of his entire life.

The day that his beloved Hena passed away was the saddest of Reb Chaim's life. The Rabbis tell us that a man calls his wife not merely by her own name, but by the name *Baisi*, My Home. When tragedy strikes and a wife passes away, a home is broken and removed from this world. Reb Chaim's home as he knew it — that home so full of love and kindness — was no more.

After all the eulogies had been delivered at her funeral, the procession wended its way to the cemetery. Everyone present was overcome by grief. The thought that this wonderful human being, this *aishes chayil*, the exemplary wife, mother and grandmother was not in our midst any longer was heart-rending. Slowly and tearfully the procession approached the final resting place of Hena, the daughter of Avraham Meyer. Her short sojourn of fifty-five years had ended. No more would her warm and comforting smile be seen; no longer would she be able to greet her beloved and cherished guests and offer them the hospitality of her home.

As the coffin was lowered into the ground, everyone was overwhelmed by sadness. When it reached the bottom of the grave, a slight movement was noticed nearby. Very few people — most of those present being preoccupied with their own grief — noticed what was happening; the action was so swift that it was barely perceived as it occurred. Reb Chaim, almost unnoticed, approached the grave and, in one motion, cast all his ledgers — which he had brought with him — into the grave.

Only later, after having had time to reflect on this remarkable deed, did we realize its profound significance. We became aware that, in truth, there were few individuals or couples as outstanding and totally devoted to each other as Chaim and Hena Gelb. Each alone was unique; together as a team they reached heights few could match. Together they built a home of charity and kindness that would be used as an example for generations to come. The casting in of the ledger was the fitting culmination to their lives as a couple. This simple action signified to the world that all good deeds he had done — the lives that Reb Chaim had touched and thereby enhanced, making people's pain more bearable and easing their hardship — were not to be credited to him alone, but this credit must be shared by this wonderful woman who was being laid to rest. All the joy and happiness he had spread were of her doing, too. The ledger books, representing thousands of charitable acts, belonged to Hena at least as much as to Reb Chaim himself, for she had sacrificed all through her life to enable her husband to come to the aid of the unfortunate. The ledger represented human aspirations, feelings, hopes and goals. Reb Chaim had penetrated the lives of these people and made them better, and the results, accomplished with Hena at his side, were hers to share forever.

Social Security

WHEN REB CHAIM WAS PAST EIGHTY years of age he became ill, and was recuperating at the home of his daughter Evelyn. He was visited by many people from every sphere of Jewish society; many institutional representatives of his acquaintance, whose organizations had benefited from Reb Chaim's generosity over the years, also came to be *mevaker choleh*.

One day a distinguished-looking gentleman arrived, a representative from one of the plethora of organizations that had received aid from Reb Chaim. He and Reb Chaim enjoyed a lengthy conversation and were deeply engrossed in each other's company. Finally this gentleman bade good-bye to Reb Chaim in his bedroom and went into the living room where Evelyn sat. She could see that he wished to bring up some subject with her, but was obviously uncomfortable and hesitant to do so. She turned to him and said, "Reb Yid, tell me what is on your mind. Don't be ashamed."

"Well," he replied, "Reb Chaim gives us his Social Security check every month, and due to his illness, we have not received it yet. We cannot exist without his support!"

Reb Chaim's daughter was stunned at hearing this, but she kept her composure and informed the gentleman that this month it was impossible to give it to him, as the entire sum had been spent on medical bills. "We'll see what we can do when he is well," she concluded. Satisfied with this, the man left.

When Evelyn informed the rest of the family about this unusual request, everyone was amazed beyond words. Our first thought was, "How did he live? This was his only source of income!" He had no savings account, as that had been depleted years before in the performing of many acts of charity. If he had been giving away his Social Security check every month, what did he have left with which to support himself? He never divulged this secret to anyone, and it remains a mystery to this day. He gave away everything he had. When he passed away, he left no bequests; his only possession was the plot of ground in which he was interred.

Chapter Six: Tzedakah

Reb Chaim speaking at a local shul's melava malkah

CHAPTER SEVEN
Chessed

Reb Chaim's Army

IT WAS AN ORDINARY *EREV SHABBOS* in Reb Chaim Gelb's house. The table was bedecked with the finest linen and the Shabbos candles were burning brightly. The table was set for eight: Reb Chaim, his wife and their four children, and two more Shabbos guests who were expected. No one had been invited specifically, but Reb Chaim usually brought two people home from *shul* on Friday night, so Hena, as a rule, set two extra places. The house was serene. The aura of Shabbos had descended, and the aromas of delicious food permeated the entire house.

Reb Chaim's three daughters sat at the table, waiting for their father and brother to return from *shul*. Hena was puttering about in the kitchen, making sure that everything was ready and in its proper place. Suddenly they all heard singing and hand-clapping from outside. This was the manner in which Reb Chaim came home every Shabbos, full of Shabbos joy and cheer. As he entered his home, he could be heard calling, "Come in, come in!" The children assumed he was speaking to the two Shabbos guests, who were sometimes shy and hesitant and needed to be coaxed into the house.

The door opened and in walked one gentleman, immediately followed by another. The family assumed that these were the two Shabbos guests. However, the door remained open, and guests

Chapter Seven: Chessed / 87

continued to stream in. In the small, crowded room it seemed as though an army had arrived, although in fact there were "only" eight additional guests. Reb Chaim showed them to their places at the table, while his daughters ran into the kitchen and quickly summoned their mother into the dining room. She had no inkling of the surprise that awaited her. She walked into the room and almost reeled backwards with shock at the unusual size of the gathering. She said a quick "Good Shabbos," and returned to the kitchen.

Reb Chaim, anticipating her dilemma, followed her into the kitchen to reassure her. "Don't worry," he told her, "just serve smaller pieces."

"You can't do that," Hena replied. "Today is Shabbos, and everyone is entitled to an adequate portion of food. This is the proper way to feed a guest." Hena had always prepared for one or two extra people at the table, but never for eight. She looked into her pots, trying to determine how many people she could feed properly.

The girls were privy to this exchange. They volunteered, "We will eat *milchig*, so you can give the guests our portions." Hena and Reb Chaim felt sorry for having to deprive them of their Shabbos meal; however, at that moment it was the only foreseeable solution. There was sufficient wine and *challah* for all; the children would then eat bananas and cream, so the Shabbos food would suffice for all the guests.

After a short consultation with his guests, Reb Chaim returned to the kitchen and announced, "Three of them also need lodging for the night." Without another thought, the girls offered, "We will sleep at a friend's house tonight; they can have our room."

When all this had been settled, Reb Chaim, his family and his guests all sat down to begin the Shabbos festivities. They all joined in the singing of *"Shalom Aleichem,"* and their voices rang out over the entire neighborhood. After all the guests had recited a beautiful *Kiddush*, and *Hamotzi* had been said over the *challah*, the meal began.

As everyone relaxed at the table, conversation began. During the discussion it was discovered that these guests were very important personages who, for various reasons, had to be away from home for Shabbos and had to seek hospitality elsewhere. One man was a *rosh yeshiva* who had come to Williamsburg to raise funds for his institution. Another was a *Rebbe* who had come to spend Shabbos in Williamsburg in celebration of an *Aufruf*, the calling up to the Torah of a bridegroom on the Shabbos before his wedding. This esteemed *Rebbe* would go to no one else's house but Reb Chaim's for Shabbos, having heard of his reputation for scrupulous observance of Shabbos and *kashrus*.

Another man was a *chazzan*, who had come for Shabbos to audition for a cantorial position in a large *shul* in the area. He delighted all present with lovely renditions of the *Kiddush* and *zemiros*. Yet another had come from *Eretz Yisrael* on the vital mission of raising funds for a seriously ill person who was unable to pay for his necessary medical treatment. The rest all had similar stories to tell. All were learned in the Torah; all had important reasons for being in Williamsburg. This became an unforgettable Shabbos. The *divrei Torah* presented at the table were enthralling and held everyone spellbound. Never had the family been present at such a gathering — let alone at their own table — with so many Torah luminaries. What had started out as a very difficult Shabbos, fraught with problems, turned out to be one of the most enjoyable ones in memory. The evening was so pleasant that no one wanted to leave the table; songs and words of Torah passed from person to person well into the night.

The children did not mind forgoing their usual Shabbos meal and giving up their room, since in return they had been treated to a Shabbos they would not soon forget. Over the years Reb Chaim continued to set an indelible example of *hachnasas orchim* for his family to follow when they grew up and had homes of their own.

Our Rabbis teach that the *mitzvah* of welcoming of guests into one's home is greater than that of talking to *Hashem*. We see this in *Parshas Vayera*, when Avraham *Avinu* was talking to *Hashem* but left Him in order to engage in the *mitzvah* of welcoming guests when the three angels, disguised as men, approached his tent. Reb Chaim could do no less than try to emulate Avraham *Avinu*; his door was always open.

The Man Who Came to Breakfast

AS WAS REB CHAIM'S CUSTOM every morning, he went to *daven shacharis* at Yeshiva Torah Vodaath, which was just around the corner from his house. One morning he returned home with a bearded young man in tow. He introduced him to Hena, and told her that he had met the man in *shul* that morning. He had recently arrived from Europe and had no relatives or friends to take him in. He was also penniless, so Reb Chaim invited him home for a good breakfast.

While Hena was serving breakfast to their guest, she was wondering, "Where will this gentleman go when he leaves here?" She called Reb Chaim aside and whispered to him, "I have something urgent to discuss with you."

She posed her question and he replied, "This matter concerns me also. This man is a fine Torah scholar and it may take him a while to settle down in America. In the meantime, do you think we can fix up a room for him here?"

Hena answered, "It shall be done," without any hesitation.

When Reb Chaim presented his proposal to the guest, the offer was readily accepted. At that moment Reb Chaim and Hena did not realize that the relationship was about to become a long-lasting one. Though this was to be only a temporary solution, the gentleman lived with them for *nine years*! He was never requested to do any work in return for his room and board, and neither was he ever charged a fee. More importantly, he was never made to feel like a burden; conversely, he was always treated as a respected member of the family.

Never Say No

IN WILLIAMSBURG THERE WAS a one-man *gemilas chessed* (free loan) society; his name was Yitzchak Aaron Kramer, the father of thirteen children who are today well known in Orthodox circles. People came from all over to borrow money from him without interest; his children today still carry on this tradition with a *gemilas chessed* society founded in his honor.

Yitzchak Aaron Kramer was Reb Chaim's best friend for many years. The following anecdote will indicate how Reb Chaim utilized Yitzchak Aaron Kramer's services in his pursuit of kindness toward his fellow Jews. One day, a man approached Reb Chaim and asked him for a loan of one thousand dollars, which he urgently required to keep his business afloat. In those days a thousand dollars was a tremendous sum, and Reb Chaim, with his own meager resources, was unable to fulfill this man's request. As usual, though, being a man of action, Reb Chaim would never turn down a supplicant. He told the man to come with him, and he quickly led him to Yitzchak Aaron Kramer's house on Penn Street in Williamsburg. The two men entered the house and, after the customary greetings, Yitzchak Aaron inquired, "Reb Chaim, what can I do for you?"

Reb Chaim replied, "This man needs one thousand dollars urgently to keep his business solvent."

"Who will be the guarantor?" asked Yitzchak Aaron.

"I will," said Reb Chaim.

Yitzchak Aaron asked, "Do you know this man?"

"No," replied Reb Chaim, "I never saw him before. He must have heard of me from others."

"Reb Chaim, how can you guarantee such a large loan for a person you don't know?"

"He will pay it back," said Reb Chaim confidently. "I will not suffer a loss in the performance of a *mitzvah*."

Yitzchak Aaron shook his head in wonder, knowing what a hardship it would impose on Reb Chaim should the man default on the loan.

This again manifests Reb Chaim's approach to doing *chessed* for his fellow Jew. A Jew in need must not be turned away; never say no!

Throughout the many years of their warm relationship, the same scene was repeated countless times. Reb Chaim brought many people to Yitzchak Aaron and guaranteed their loans, and suffered little or no loss in the process.

A PENNILESS ISRAELI FAMILY had arrived in America and moved to Williamsburg. They had no relatives or friends in this country. No one was aware of their situation and, being new to the country, they were shy, uninformed and fearful; they did not know where to turn for help. None of their neighbors was aware of their severe economic ordeal. They actually did not have money with which to buy food! They were baffled and unschooled in the ways of the new world in which they found themselves. To whom could they turn for assistance?

Helping the Helpless

One day there was an unexpected knock at their door. In came Reb Chaim, laden with food and money. To this family he was like an angel sent from heaven in answer to their prayers. How had he found out about them? No organization, with all their skilled help and large offices, had records of this family's arrival and their needs. No one knew of any specific method Reb Chaim had for rooting out the indigent; it was like a sixth sense to him. Like a homing pigeon, he arrived at the needed spot.

From that day on, he was a regular visitor to their home. He raised their spirits and counseled them on finding jobs, schools and the like. He helped them to establish themselves in their new home; today, they are able to do the same for others.

TODAY, FORTUNATELY, there are many communities in which we find *bikur cholim* organizations, whose sole purpose is to visit the sick and aid them as necessary. During the pre-World War II years and for many of the years that followed, however, virtually none of these organizations existed. Individuals who wanted to participate in this vital *mitzvah* had to do it on their own.

Bikur Cholim

Here again, whenever the opportunity presented itself, Reb Chaim was there to help. He made it his business to visit hospitals and take care of the sick. One particular incident in his observance of this *mitzvah* stands out. A *frum* acquaintance of his became seriously ill and, due to circumstances beyond his control, was placed in a non-kosher hospital, with no kosher facilities available.

In those days kosher precooked meals were not on the market, either. Being observant of the laws of *kashrus*, this man refused to partake of the meals served to him in the hospital. When Reb Chaim became aware of his predicament, he and his wife immediately took action. Hena cooked chicken and soup, which Reb Chaim delivered to the sick man at the hospital. It was a long trip and it took him the better part of a day, but Reb Chaim did it at least three times a week during the patient's entire hospital stay. He did it cheerfully, uncomplainingly, and with love, and managed to accomplish this feat without neglecting his other *maasim tovim*.

Chessed Par Excellence

THIS STORY WAS RELATED TO ME by Shalom Greenzweig, a gentleman I met at a wedding. A young *Chassid* and his family were invited to a wedding. The man did not own a car, and he went to the wedding with his family by public transportation. The wedding was lively and beautiful, and the festivities lasted late into the night. Finally the wedding drew to a close, and everyone began preparing to leave. Most of the celebrants headed for their cars for the trip home. Reb Chaim was waiting for his ride home when he spotted the young *Chassid* and his family leaving the wedding hall, walking along the deserted streets. Reb Chaim approached the man and asked, "Where are you going? Where is your car?"

The *Chassid* replied, "I have no car. We are going home by subway, the same way we arrived."

Reb Chaim retorted, "By subway so late at night? It is too long and dangerous a ride for you and your children! Wait, I'll get you a ride."

Reb Chaim positioned himself at the exit of the parking lot and stopped the first car he saw. "Listen, you must do this *mitzvah*. There is a family with young children stranded here. You must take them home!"

"Which way are they going?" asked the driver.

"To Williamsburg," replied Reb Chaim.

"Sorry," said the driver, "I'm going to Queens."

Chapter Seven: Chessed / 93

Reb Chaim reluctantly let him drive on. He stopped the next car and again was turned down, because that car was already full. Undaunted, Reb Chaim maintained his post and continued to stop one car after another, without success. There was always an excuse not to accommodate this family. But Reb Chaim did not give up. After about twenty-five cars had turned him down, he was finally successful in finding a ride for the *Chassid* and his family. Reb Chaim never was one to stint on the time or effort needed for the performance of *chessed* towards any individual.

Who Has a Scythe?

THINGS CHANGE IN JEWISH LIFE as they do in the secular world. I don't mean *halachah* — that is immutable. What I am referring to here is the mode of our lives today. Computers now can check *sifrei Torah* to see if they are written properly according to *halachah*, and do a better job than the human eye. Prefabricated *succos* are another modern development. In previous times people would build their *succos* out of old doors or other scrap wood; today, one can use panels especially constructed for this purpose.

S'chach for the roof of the *succah* must be made of something that grew from the ground and could not become unclean. In New York today, bamboo, which is not perishable, is commonly used; in previous times, the most frequently used substance for *s'chach* was the reeds that grew along the water. They were tall and solid, and could cover large areas of the *succah*. One of the favorite harvesting grounds for these reeds was the wetlands of Canarsie, where they were in plentiful supply. Before the *Succos* holiday there emerged a group of entrepreneurs who dealt in this product and earned much-needed money for the holiday.

The following was related to me by Alexander Weinreb, a prominent Boro Park businessman and a contemporary of mine at the Yeshiva Chofetz Chaim. He and another *bachur*, Yochanan Chait, who is now a prominent rabbi in Mount Vernon, decided to go into business selling *s'chach* before *Succos*. This was a way for them to raise money to enable them to continue learning at the yeshiva. However, they had no money to buy the necessary tools with which to cut the *s'chach*. Where could they get a scythe? How many people in the city possess one? Whom could they ask for this vital instrument? They inquired around and were told that Reb Chaim Gelb owned one. They approached him with trepidation, as they had never even met him. Would a total stranger lend them such a valuable tool? Would he see them? Would they be refused? They approached Reb Chaim, who greeted them warmly. When he was apprised of their request he immediately responded in the affirmative, stating, "You wish to supply the people of Williamsburg with *s'chach*? A *mitzvah* such as this is of great importance. Certainly, my friends, you may have the scythe." With the broad smile and sunny countenance that were his trademark, he gave them the scythe, without any conditions, nothing asked or requested. He wished them great success.

Forty years later, Al Weinreb remembers this incident vividly, owing to the scope of the *chessed* performed and the manner in which it was executed. Reb Chaim's goodness and sincerity evoked a similar response from all who dealt with him.

A Tragedy

REB YOM TOV PRULICK lived in Canton, Massachusetts, a small town outside Boston. He was one of the few *shomrei Shabbos* in that town, and was a fervent follower of the Bostoner *Rebbe*, *z"l*. When his son Mordechai reached *bar-mitzvah* age and was ready to enter high school, he was sent to Williamsburg to attend Mesivta Torah Vodaath, where he became an excellent student.

Reb Yom Tov arranged for his son to be a boarder in the home of Mr. and Mrs. Goldman, who were Reb Chaim's tenants, living in an upper floor of his house. Reb Yom Tov was happy, Mordechai was happy, and everything was going along smoothly. Mordechai was invited to Reb Chaim's house for many Shabbos meals as well.

Suddenly, out of the blue, Mordechai was struck by a life-threatening illness, which was diagnosed as mastoiditis. Today this disease can be easily cured with the administration of antibiotics, but these life-saving drugs had not yet been discovered at that time. The disease, if it reached the brain, could prove fatal.

The Goldmans were elderly people and could not give Mordechai all the care he required. Often Reb Chaim and Hena stepped in and became surrogate parents to the sick child. Hena stayed up many nights with Mordechai, giving him his medicine and taking care of him. Reb Chaim took him to a number of different doctors and specialists. He began to get better, but one *Yom Tov* he suddenly took a turn for the worse and had to be hospitalized immediately. Hena immediately sent him with her son Avigdor, by cab to the hospital, as Reb Chaim was in *shul* at the time. Unfortunately, Mordechai never recovered and was *niftar* at the age of fifteen. His heartbroken parents, who had not spared any efforts in trying to save their child, were devastated. They had been *mosrei nefesh*, self-sacrificing, so that their child could learn Torah — only to be hit with such a tragedy!

They were strong in their faith, however, and never deviated one iota from it. They were thankful to the Gelbs for their devotion to their beloved departed son, and remained lifelong friends with them. They established a *gemilas chessed* fund in *Eretz Yisrael* in memory of Mordechai.

Chessed Shel Emes — True Kindness

IT WAS A WELL-KNOWN FACT in Williamsburg that in cases of dire emergencies, when no one else was available for assistance, the yeshiva could always be relied on to supply help. Therefore, it was not too surprising when one day Yeshiva Torah Vodaath received a call stating that a Jew had passed away in Rockland County, north of the city, and there was no one to take care of his burial and funeral needs. In Jewish law, this is called a *mes mitzvah*. If no one would come forward to assist with the burial, they were told, he would be buried in Potter's Field, owned by New York and used for the interment of paupers who could not afford private burial. Of course this option was completely unacceptable. Under Jewish law, a Jew must be buried in consecrated ground, in a Jewish cemetery. It was fortunate that someone in the hospital in Rockland County knew something about the law, and had the presence of mind to call the yeshiva for help. When the people who were gathered there heard about this situation, they stopped what they were doing and came together to discuss how to handle the problem. Reb Chaim, being a regular worshiper at the yeshiva, was there that day too. Everyone racked their brains trying to think of people with the same last name as the deceased to see if he had any relatives, but it was to no avail. No one knew of any family that this poor man might have had.

Someone also pointed out that there was the imminent threat of an autopsy being performed by the hospital staff. Since the individual had no relatives and his hospital bill was unpaid, the hospital could exercise its rights to perform an autopsy, which would again be contrary to Jewish law. The deceased had no one to stand up for him and oppose an autopsy; this was another problem that had to be resolved forthwith.

The case seemed hopeless. Everyone was becoming more and more agitated by the minute, but no plan of action was being developed. All at once, Reb Chaim stood up and said, "I will undertake this project. I will go out myself and do what is necessary to overcome these obstacles."

The room became silent for a moment. Then the commotion resumed as the synagogue became alive with loud chatter and comments.

"He'll never be able to do it!" said one.

Another questioned, "Where will he get the money to pay for the funeral?"

Still another asked, "What authority does he have to prevent an autopsy?"

Others shouted, "There is not enough time! It is a long trip to Rockland County, and by the time you get there the hospital will have already made all the decisions."

As the clamor in the synagogue continued, an individual came running in, shouting, "Do you see what's going on outside? A winter storm has started, and the snow is piling up fast. How will you ever be able to drive out there in such weather?"

Reb Chaim managed to call the group to order and asked, "Is there anyone else here who wishes to volunteer?" Not a whisper was heard. Everyone felt it was an impossible mission. Reb Chaim then repeated, "Since there are no other volunteers, I take it upon myself to do this sacred task. I will make sure to get the job done."

He paused for a moment, and then his final statement shocked the already stunned crowd even more. "I also promise all of you gathered here that I will say the *Kaddish* for this *niftar* for the entire year."

Reb Chaim quickly removed his *tallis* and *tefillin* and carefully packed them away. He left with the words, "If you'll excuse me, I must get started on my way."

He immediately reached a telephone and dialed the number of a very good friend, a well-known and influential member of the Williamsburg community. Fortunately Reb Chaim found him at home, as the snowstorm had hindered him from going out that day. The man recognized Reb Chaim's voice right away. "What can I do for you today, Reb Chaim?"

"It's a matter of life or death, Reb Yaakov — you must help!"

"Life or death? Everything is a matter of life or death with you!"

"No, no!" emphasized Reb Chaim. "This truly is a matter of life or death, Reb Yaakov! A man has died without leaving a family, and there is a real threat of an autopsy being performed, and of his being buried in Potter's Field."

Reb Yaakov knew many prominent politicians and community figures who could open many doors for him. They all respected him because they knew that all the requests he made of them came from the goodness of his heart, and Reb Yaakov himself spent much time and energy on these good works. He told Reb Chaim, "I'll make some calls and see what I can do. You wait there, and when I'm through I'll come over and meet you."

About twenty minutes later Reb Yaakov burst breathlessly into the room. He ran over to Reb Chaim and told him, "The autopsy is off. I assumed responsibility for the burial — that of course means you too, as we're in this together."

Reb Chaim replied, "While you were busy at your end, I was

busy on mine. I called up my burial society and spoke to the president. When I told him this sad story he said that the society would inter the deceased free of charge in their plot. Now all we have to do is make the funeral arrangements and get a rabbi to officiate."

At that moment Rabbi Leib walked in; when he heard the story, he immediately agreed to participate. "Of course I will officiate. This is a *mes mitzvah*."

Reb Yaakov called the funeral parlor to make arrangements for the funeral. He quickly informed the person who answered the phone what was required in this emergency. This person informed Reb Yaakov that although the proprietor was not in, he himself would take care of the arrangements and would send a hearse out later.

Reb Yaakov then noted, "We must get out to Rockland State Hospital as soon as we can to make sure that everything is being carried out according to our wishes and expectations. We can't rely on the proper things being done without our being there personally to supervise."

They stepped out of the yeshiva and into the raging snowstorm. The only mode of transportation to Rockland County they could think of was a taxi; but how to get a taxi in such weather? None was in sight. They stood peering into the swirling snowflakes hoping for a miracle. Finally, after about five minutes, a yellow cab appeared. They flagged the cab down and jumped in. "Rockland State Hospital, and hurry!" said Reb Chaim.

"Are you out of your mind?" the cab driver retorted. "In such a storm? I wouldn't take you there for a thousand dollars!"

Reb Chaim entreated, "But this is a matter of life and death!" He quickly related the details pertaining to the matter at hand; this was the final step of their project.

The cabbie said, "You call this life or death? He's dead already! What's so bad if he's buried in Potter's Field?"

Reb Yaakov and Reb Chaim both tried to explain the religious aspects to the cabbie, but to no avail. Although the driver was Jewish, he was unschooled and illiterate in Jewish law and learning. They were beginning to despair of ever reaching their destination.

Suddenly the cab driver said to them, "You guys must be getting a pretty penny for this adventure."

Reb Chaim and Reb Yaakov were forced to laugh. "Pretty penny? It's costing us money! We're doing it for the sake of a *mitzvah*, a good deed!"

When the cabbie heard this, he changed his mind and agreed to join them in their mission. "For nothing? You guys are heroes! All right, I'll be a hero too." A spark had been aroused in him.

They started off on their journey through the deserted streets. As the taxi driver laboriously made his way through the snow, he thought to himself, "What a fool I am! Here I was headed for home and a hot breakfast and a relaxing day in a cozy warm house. Now I find myself out in a freezing, dangerous storm. What will I tell my wife? She'll think I'm completely out of my mind! All of a sudden I'm doing *mitzvos*. *Meshuga*, crazy, that's what she'll say. How did I ever let these two people talk me into this?"

In the back of the cab Reb Chaim and Reb Yaakov were discussing all the work that remained to be done. All activities had to be coordinated so that the funeral would take place properly and all possible pitfalls would be avoided. They were aware that everything had to work perfectly. The autopsy must be canceled. The undertaker must send out the hearse in time. The burial society must make all the necessary arrangements for the interment. Everything had to run smoothly, even in the face of this severe snowstorm.

Reb Chaim said to the cab driver, "*Hashem* is testing us to see whether we have the proper *mesiras nefesh* to help a fellow Jew, especially one who cannot help himself. Usually when one performs a good deed for his fellow Jew, there is the possibility of the recipient performing a kindness for him in return. But in this case there is no way that the doer of the good deed will be repaid by the recipient. This is a *chessed shel emes*, a true kindness."

The trip continued uneventfully. Reb Chaim recited *Tehillim* and Reb Yaakov occupied himself with a volume of *Mishnah*. There was no time for frivolity, and time was of the essence.

Suddenly they were startled as the driver gave a loud gasp. They felt the cab skid on an icy patch of road. What the two men in the back seat could not see — and the reason for the cabbie's gasp — was that the taxi was headed directly towards a tree in its path! The driver tried his utmost to maneuver the taxi away from the tree, and managed to stop the car only a few inches away from it. Reb Chaim and Reb Yaakov immediately called to mind the words of our Sages, who said that when a person is engaged in performing a *mitzvah*, no harm will befall him.

They resumed their journey, and finally reached Rockland State Hospital. The driver got out to stretch his legs and relax, but Reb Chaim and Reb Yaakov had no time to waste. They did not pause for a second, but rushed into the hospital and asked at the information desk for the doctor who Reb Yaakov had been told would be in charge of all the arrangements.

The doctor, who had been contacted by Reb Yaakov's friend, came down to greet the two men. He told them that everything had been taken care of. The autopsy order had been remanded, and he would release the body to the undertaker. The only thing left to do was wait for the hearse.

Reb Chaim exclaimed, "*Baruch Hashem*, thank G-d that everything has worked out so well! But I just recalled that I promised to say *Kaddish* for the deceased for the entire year. It's almost time for *minchah*, and there is no *minyan* here. What shall I do?"

Reb Yaakov said to him, "I will wait here and go back with the undertaker. You return now with the taxi driver, go right to the yeshiva and round up a *minyan*. Get started now, and I will take care of everything when the undertaker comes." Reb Chaim left, but the drama at the hospital was not yet over. The hearse arrived promptly, but the body was nowhere to be found. A search was conducted and the body was located in the pathology department where autopsies were performed. Someone had not been aware that the decision to perform an autopsy had been revoked, and the body was being readied for the procedure. Fortunately it was found in time. The *niftar* was placed in the hearse and Reb Yaakov went along to make sure nothing else went wrong.

Everything worked out perfectly. Reb Chaim said the *Kaddish* with more than his usual fervor, which invoked an equal response from the assembled worshipers. The cab driver, who stayed to complete the *minyan*, was no longer bitter at being kept out in the storm. He warmly said to Reb Chaim, "Now I can understand why you *frum* Jews perform *mitzvos*. The pleasure you derive from their performance cannot be matched by anything."

A Neighbor Recalls Reb Chaim's Kindness

IN RESPONSE TO THE OPEN LETTER I had printed in *The Jewish Press*, in which I solicited anecdotes and personal memories about Reb Chaim Gelb, the following reply arrived from Mrs. Beverly Zuckerman Rabinowitz:

"I am a product of Williamsburg, having lived there from the time of my birth until I was seventeen. My parents, my sister and I moved from there to Canarsie in February, 1956. From the time I was about three years old until we left Williamsburg, we had lived at 218 Division Avenue, the same street on which the Gelbs lived. Our house was directly across the street from their bakery.

"I fondly remember Chaim Gelb as somewhat of a neighborhood 'character.' I can still picture him in my mind, walking (always rapidly) around the neighborhood wearing his *tallis kattan* and holding his ever-present *pushka*. He stopped to speak to anyone who would listen, and even those who were in a hurry seemed able to make time to stop and listen. Those hearing him for the first time, I think, were somewhat surprised to hear him speak in unaccented English. I especially remember two incidents representative of his outstanding and unselfish generosity and *tzedakah*.

"In the early morning hours of May 19, 1944, on Friday, as I've been told, my mother went into labor. I was only five and one-half years old at the time, so I do not personally recollect the incident. However, my mother and my late father related the story on so many occasions that I almost consider it part of my own personal store of memories. At that time we did not have a telephone, and my father kept leaving our apartment — first to go to a nearby phone to call the doctor, and eventually to try to find a cab. Needless to say, there were not many cruising taxis at about 5 a.m. Reb Chaim Gelb suddenly appeared and, seeing my father, asked where he was going at that hour of the morning. When the situation was explained, Reb Chaim said that a cab would be arriving shortly, since every Friday he ordered one to take him to pick up *challos* for his bakery. He insisted that my parents take his taxi, since he considered their mission much more important than his own. The cab driver obliged and drove my parents to the hospital in Manhattan, where my beautiful baby sister was born only a few hours later.

"I cannot recall the exact date of the second incident — it was a frigid winter morning sometime in the late 1940's when a house around the corner from us, on Ross Street between Lee and Division Avenues, began to burn. Several fire engines were summoned to the scene, and many firefighters battled the blaze. It was a bitter cold day. I have a vivid memory of Reb Chaim Gelb rushing back and forth (I don't recall him ever walking slowly!) with hot coffee for the firemen. Although I cannot say so with certainty, I would venture to guess that he even brought them some cake or cookies from his bakery.*

"We were privileged to renew our acquaintance with Chaim Gelb's youngest daughter, Rose Rosenberg, during the last years of her life. We were members of the same *shul*, Congregation Beth Tikvah in Canarsie. She was a wonderful person and I have no doubt that her warm personality was, at least in part, influenced by her father's love, warm feelings, and generosity towards all people."

---

* This incident is discussed in greater detail later in this book.

Chapter Seven: Chessed / 103

CHAPTER EIGHT
Supporting Torah

IN DR. GERSHON KRANZLER'S TRIBUTE to Reb Chaim Gelb "The 'Oisher' of Williamsburg" [*The Jewish Observer*, November, 1981], he relates an incident in which an acquaintance had been involved many years ago. This individual — then known as Yankeleh — had been sent out of his class in Yeshiva Torah Vodaath because his family was unable to pay tuition. Although the yeshiva wanted to admit anyone who wanted to attend, it was strapped for funds to pay the *rebbeim*, and was unable to extend scholarships. The young student was sobbing in the hallway when Reb Chaim spotted him and asked what calamity had occurred to make him cry so bitterly. The boy could hardly speak, but Reb Chaim understood the problem right away. He marched directly to the school office, pulled out a few dollars, and told the administrator that he would personally be responsible for the child's tuition until Yankeleh's parents could pay again. He demanded that the boy be let back into class. The administrator gladly complied. In the days of the Depression times were bad, and there were numerous cases similar to the one that Dr. Kranzler mentioned. The small amount of money needed for tuition was an overwhelming sum to many, but Reb Chaim was able to help many young boys continue their Torah education and become Torah scholars.

Support for Torah Institutions and Students

Some years ago, Reb Chaim's granddaughter went to enroll her son in a prominent, popular yeshiva. This particular school is quite renowned in the Jewish world, and it is therefore very difficult to gain admission; often people are turned away due to lack of space. The yeshiva is thus highly selective because of the great demand for seats. When Reb Chaim's granddaughter told the dean of the school about their kinship to Reb Chaim, her child was immediately accepted.

Why this immediate decision? The dean revealed to her an incident of which she had not been aware:

"It was very difficult to start a yeshiva many years ago, when we established this school. Although we now have a flourishing, thriving educational institution, when we began, we had just a few students and almost no money. On the opening day of the new yeshiva, in walked Reb Chaim. I knew him well, and we greeted each other warmly. Reb Chaim wished us success, then took out some money. He handed it to me and remarked, 'A yeshiva needs students, but it also needs money. You know what it says in *Pirkei Avos*: *Im ain kemach, ain Torah* — If there is no flour, there can be no Torah.'

"This donation was the first that our fledgling yeshiva received from any individual," continued the dean, "and that one act gave us more strength and courage to continue our efforts than did many larger donations in the years that followed."

Then he added, "Is there any doubt that Reb Chaim Gelb's great-grandchild would be admitted as a student here? I welcome him with open arms in the same spirit in which Reb Chaim opened his arms to us and gave us help when we needed it most."

THE FOLLOWING ANECDOTE was related to me by Jack J. Nelson:

Rabbi Mendlowitz's Visit

"During the 1930's, on Division Avenue in the Williamsburg section of Brooklyn, stood the *Polisher shtiebl*, which had approximately three hundred members.

"The *Polisher shtiebl* was very active in charitable work. As this was the time before unemployment insurance, welfare, social security and health insurance, the *Gemilas Chessed* Committee of the *Polisher shtiebl* certainly had its hands full.

"This committee met periodically in my house. They would schedule the weekly Shabbos appeal for yeshivos, rabbis, organizations, and people in financial difficulty. They would find jobs for people so they would not have to work on Saturday, and get cosigners for bank loans so that Jews could open grocery stores and thus not have to work on the Sabbath.

"I was a little boy at the time and would eavesdrop, listening to the interesting, heart-rending stories.

"In lighter moments they would talk with scorn about some of those people who went around collecting on their own, and who gave no accounting of the sums solicited. As a prime example they picked on Reb Chaim Gelb. What does he do with all the money that he goes around collecting all day? Big deal! So he gives the kids a penny each to entice them to go into *shul* and answer 'Amen.' Big deal!

"One day it got back to the committee that Reb Shraga Feivel Mendlowitz, the prestigious *rosh yeshiva* of the Mesivta Torah Vodaath, honored Reb Chaim Gelb by accepting his invitation to eat *seudah shlishis* at his house. The committee members flew into a jealous furor at hearing this. 'How does this *meshugana* who stands on the corner of Division and Marcy on Friday afternoons telling the passing women to light Shabbos candles rate such *kavod*?'

"Eventually the facts came out: Reb Chaim Gelb had single-handedly raised thousands of dollars to help keep the doors of this great Torah-learning institution open during the Depression years!

"Thirty-five years later, having to say *Kaddish*, if I missed the morning services I could still catch a *minyan* at the yeshiva on Wilson Street on my way to work. Reb Chaim Gelb was still there soliciting funds. I would give him a ten-dollar bill and say, 'Here is your penny back, plus interest.'"

IN THE EARLY DAYS OF YESHIVA TORAH VODAATH, there were many instances where the yeshiva was unable to meet its payroll on time. They then used a tactic utilized by many yeshivas, the issuing of "head checks." These were checks that were post-dated several weeks ahead. But a *rebbe* could usually not wait several weeks to cash his check; he had his bills to pay, too. He had to find a kind-hearted individual who would lay out the amount of money on the face of the check, and then hold the check until its date. In the meantime, the *rebbe* would have money to feed his family and pay his bills. Reb Chaim was always willing to lay out the cash to cover these "head checks" to help the *rebbeim*, and the yeshiva, over the hump.

The Post-Dated Checks

Reb Chaim never publicly boasted or bragged about his good deeds. He quietly went about doing what he "had" to do. His *maasim tovim* were well known to the recipients of these good works, however. It was not for nothing that Rabbi Mendlowitz honored Reb Chaim with many visits; he was fully aware of all of Reb Chaim's efforts on behalf of that institution in general and each *rebbe* in particular. Although he accomplished all his good deeds without fanfare, Reb Chaim was one of the strongest supporters of the yeshiva.

IN THE 1940'S THERE WERE VERY FEW post-high school students or *bais medrash* students studying in the various yeshivos. The *kollel* as we know it today was almost non-existent; there were only two yeshivos supporting and conducting *kollels* at that time. I had the privilege of being a member of the first *kollel* group of the Yeshiva Chofetz Chaim of Williamsburg; we had a total of four students.

Supporting a Son-in-Law

The concept of the need to produce great Torah scholars had not yet taken root in this country. Perhaps it was too soon to feel the results of the Holocaust in the field of Torah. Promulgation of Torah knowledge for select post-graduate work was not as well received among the religious society as it is today. The concept of a *kollel* was European in origin; many of the *gedolim* of both the

Chapter Eight: Supporting Torah / 107

previous generation and of our time had graduated from *kollel* and gone on to establish yeshivos of their own.

In view of the surrounding circumstances, it was unusual that when Reb Chaim's daughter became engaged to a *bachur* at the Yeshiva Chofetz Chaim, Rabbi Chaim Pinchas Scheinberg, the *mashgiach* of the yeshiva (now world-renowned dean of Yeshiva Torah Ohr in *Eretz Yisrael*), asked the *chassan* to remain in the yeshiva and learn for two years after his marriage.

In view of the financial situation of the Gelb family, this seemed like an unattainable goal. As the owners of the first *shomer Shabbos* bakery in Williamsburg, the Gelbs barely made ends meet. However, without bickering or undue discussion, they readily agreed to this proposition. Reb Chaim felt that it would be a great *zechus*, merit, for him to support a son-in-law who was studying Torah. Although he himself had never been afforded this opportunity, his children would receive every chance they could to scale the heights of Torah study. He supported his daughter's husband with honor and respect, never allowing the young couple to feel in the slightest way that it was a burden for him to support them.

The investment paid off handsomely: The benefits are the scores of Reb Chaim's children, grandchildren and great-grandchildren who have spent their lives pursuing the paths of Torah.

One day I was sitting in his home when he came over to me and said, "Thank you."

I looked up, startled, wondering what I had done to deserve his thanks.

Again he repeated, "Thank you, Dovid."

As hard as I tried, I could not recall a recent event or task I had performed that would warrant his thanks.

He seemed to understand my quandary, and expanded further, "Thank you for what you are doing for my family."

I racked my brains in the attempt to recall what I had done for them, but to no avail. My mind remained blank.

"For learning Torah," he concluded — and the mystery was solved.

I couldn't believe my ears. *He* earnestly felt gratitude towards *me* for studying Torah! Reb Chaim meant this sincerely; he never spoke lightly.

Many people today proudly and willingly support their children in their pursuit of Torah. But how many feel that by doing so they owe a debt of gratitude to the people they are supporting and not the other way around? It is true that the children being supported must be thankful to their parents. However, how many parents will tell their children, "Thank you for learning Torah. You are doing me a favor and I owe you thanks"? A donor who was thankful to the recipient — that's the kind of person that Reb Chaim was.

CHAPTER NINE
Children

Moshele's Glasses

MOSHELE WAS SLOWLY WALKING down Wilson Street in Williamsburg, on his way to yeshiva. He was a fourth grader, and his mind was occupied with various thoughts concerning his class and classmates.

He was still angry at his classmate, Shloime, who was always calling out answers in class. Moshele was a bright boy but was also quite shy. He never thrust himself forward to be noticed by the *rebbe*, but he tried to make a good impression nonetheless. Shloime, on the other hand, always attempted to gather all the glory for himself. Just the day before, Moshele had raised his hand to answer a difficult question when Shloime blurted out the answer before Moshele had had a chance to be recognized.

Although he was hurt by the actions of his classmate, Moshele tried to find a reason for Shloime's behavior. Perhaps, he thought, it was because Shloime was away from his family that he was constantly seeking attention from his *rebbe*. Shloime's parents lived in a small town far away, where no Jewish education was available, so, at the age of six, Shloime had been sent to Williamsburg to live at the yeshiva. Moshele was a good-hearted child and could not harbor resentment against anyone for any length of time, and so he was not about to hold a grudge against Shloime, either.

As he walked, enveloped in his thoughts, he took off his glasses to wipe them clean. Suddenly, out of nowhere, someone barreled into him and knocked his glasses from his hand.

Moshele stooped to pick up his glasses and was faced by tragedy: His glasses were broken! As he began to recover from this shock, he was hit with the realization that the boy who had run into him was none other than his nemesis, Shloime. Shloime had been playing ball, and was chasing an errant grounder when, without looking where he was going, he bumped into Moshele.

Moshele glanced unbelievingly at Shloime, his mouth agape. "No, no," he thought, "not only did he deprive me of my rightful honor in class, now he also comes along and does me harm!" He burst into uncontrollable tears, the rage he felt about his glasses being broken mingling with the anger of the previous day.

At that moment the bell rang, signaling that classes were about to begin. The boys lined up and went to class. Moshele was so devastated, however, that he could do nothing but remain behind in tears. The double injury was just too much for him, and he could not bring himself to stop crying and go up to his class.

As his tears subsided, Moshele's thoughts became more rational but no less frightening. How could he confront his parents with the unfortunate loss of his glasses? They had only been purchased recently, after his *rebbe* noticed that he had trouble reading from the blackboard and informed his parents that without glasses his progress in learning would be severely impeded. Standing there, holding the mangled glasses in his hands, Moshele could vividly picture how his parents would look when they found out what had befallen him. Moshele's parents were working-class people, trying to pull themselves out of the grip of the Depression. Scraping together enough money to buy the glasses had meant a tremendous sacrifice; how would they ever be able to pay for another pair?

Just then, who should come by but Reb Chaim. He spotted the sobbing boy and approached him, inquiring as to what had occurred. Wordlessly, Moshele showed him his damaged spectacles and then explained how it all had happened.

Chapter Nine: Children / 111

"How can I go home now and face my parents with this?" he sobbed.

Reb Chaim needed no further elaboration, as he well understood the family's financial situation. "Come with me," he said to Moshele. "Let's see what can be done." He took Moshele's hand and they quietly walked along together. Moshele knew Reb Chaim, as did everyone in the neighborhood, but he had no clue as to what Reb Chaim's actions would be. He just went docilely along with him.

After walking for about fifteen minutes Reb Chaim said, "Here we are." They entered a store, and Moshele immediately recognized it as an optician's. His heart leapt into his mouth as he realized what Reb Chaim was about to do. Reb Chaim turned to the optician and said, "This is an emergency. This boy cannot afford to miss learning Torah. Please fix these glasses at once."

The optician, who knew Reb Chaim, did not resist at all. He put aside all his other duties and set to work repairing Moshele's glasses. "Yes," he said, "the world rests on the learning of our youth. This is a real emergency."

When the glasses were finished at last, he tried them on Moshele and they fit perfectly. Moshele's face lit up with happiness and he hugged Reb Chaim and the optician with thanks.

"Off with you, my little *tzaddik*. Get back to your Torah learning!" said Reb Chaim, and Moshele, his step much lighter, went down the street and in through the doors of his beloved yeshiva.

Brachos Can Win the War

AS ONE READS THIS BOOK, one can observe a singular factor in the life of Reb Chaim. Although he was not an educator by profession, he did have great influence upon others. Whereas the average person in his lifetime usually touches the lives of only his immediate family and perhaps a small circle of friends, Reb Chaim literally affected the lives of thousands of people, some in a minor fashion and others very significantly. Whoever came into contact with him felt the magnetism of his presence. Many retained the memories of their meetings, fleeting though they had been, for many years afterward. Twenty or thirty years later, these people still had their fond memories of Reb Chaim.

Although he held no official job, Reb Chaim never rested. He spent many more hours working for *klal Yisrael* than most workingmen holding regular jobs spend at their work. He never ceased his activities, giving and collecting *tzedakah*, traveling to hospitals, and visiting widows and orphans. His constant presence in every location at which people gathered to do *mitzvos* made him well known. The contacts he had with these thousands of people made a great impact on them.

As mentioned, although Reb Chaim was not a rabbi or teacher by profession, he did serve to educate many others. He was particularly noted for his activity around the yeshiva during the daily recess and before school.

The students at Yeshiva Torah Vodaath had a long day in school, beginning at about nine A.M. and concluding at about six P.M. They worked very hard and tried to use any free time they had for good purposes. Reb Chaim, who lived around the corner from the yeshiva, was always there to greet the boys warmly.

When the children came out of yeshiva for their break, they were always ravenous. A knish vendor had set up his cart in front of the yeshiva building, and he did a thriving business with the yeshiva students. A knish cost five cents then, and Reb Chaim would stand by the knish vendor's cart giving free knishes to those who could not afford to pay the nickel. He would spot a boy standing apart from the group and say to him, "Yossele, did you eat anything for lunch today?"

If the boy responded in the negative, Reb Chaim would say, "Come here!" He would go over to the knish vendor, buy a knish, and give it to the hungry boy. He then would raise his hand for silence, like a teacher in the classroom. "Everyone be quiet while he makes a *brachah!*" he would announce. "We must all answer 'Amen' after this *brachah*. Our Rabbis say that he who answers 'Amen' after a *brachah* gets more of a reward that the one who makes the *brachah*." Like an orchestra leader, he led the children

Chapter Nine: Children / 113

in the performance of this *mitzvah*. He conducted the recital of the *brachah* and the answering of *'Amen'* with precision and with *kavanah* (feeling).

When he finished with Yossele he would find a Shimmie or a Yitzchak. There was never a shortage of hungry boys, and all were willing and enthusiastic about participating in this activity. The blessings were loud and clear, and the *Amens* even louder. This "*mitzvah* project" had a great deal of influence on the participants, who related these anecdotes to me years later. By his devotion, sincerity and dedication, Reb Chaim made an indelible impression on these young minds.

During World War II, when America was engaged in a struggle with its vicious enemies, Reb Chaim employed another tactic to motivate the children to make their *brachos* with enthusiasm. "You know," he would tell them, "the Japanese and Germans are good fighters and good pilots. Our aviators are up against very capable and trained opponents. You can understand the danger our boys are in, and that the enemy they confront is a tough one. They need all the help they can get!"

"But what can *we* do to help them?" they would ask. "They are overseas fighting the war, and we are here in Williamsburg, in yeshiva. We are thousands of miles from them!"

Reb Chaim anticipated this question. He stated simply, "Every *brachah* that we make will enable us to shoot down an enemy plane."

The children looked at him in amazement. They could participate in the war without actually being in the combat arena? They could fight the enemy and win! This was a startling revelation.

"When we do *Hashem's* will, He does our will," Reb Chaim continued. "What is our will? To win the war! *Hashem* will be on our side because we make our *brachos* and do *mitzvos*."

The children were astonished; they had never thought about *brachos* in this fashion before now. Reb Chaim had brought an important lesson home to them. The children responded with great spirit and warmth. Their *brachos* became louder and more powerful than ever. This lesson did not only serve that particular purpose at that moment, but those who heard it would remember Reb Chaim's admonition throughout their lives: "Make a *brachah*, and shoot down an enemy plane!" If we do *mitzvos*, *Hashem* will remember us and help us.

Reb Chaim's Gift

REFAEL SHAIN AND HIS BROTHER GERSHON were walking on Division Avenue past Reb Chaim's bakery, when suddenly the door opened and Reb Chaim called them in. They were young students at Yeshiva Torah Vodaath at that time. They became excited because they knew that Reb Chaim gave out candies and other food items so that the children should make the blessings over them; they eagerly entered the bakery, anticipating a cookie or a piece of cake.

Instead of receiving a goodie, however, the two boys were told that Reb Chaim was going to make a *brachah*, and he wanted them to answer "Amen." Refael told me that even after forty years, he vividly recalls that dramatic moment and can visualize how Reb Chaim made his *brachah*. Every word was uttered with *kavanah* (feeling), sincerity and emotion; each word came from the center of his being.

Even after witnessing this awe-inspiring recitation of the *brachah*, the boys were disappointed at not receiving a piece of cake themselves, and thus answered "Amen" in low, quiet voices. Reb Chaim reprimanded them for this, saying that "Amen" should be said loudly. He noticed the look of disappointment on their faces, however, and went on to tell them, "Look, boys. The Rabbis say that whoever answers 'Amen' to a blessing is greater than the one who makes the blessing. You children are getting a greater reward than I am."

As they turned to go, Reb Chaim called the children back. "Now it's your turn to make a *brachah*," he told Refael with a smile, "and we will answer 'Amen.'" He held out a cookie to the child, who accepted it happily, made a loud *brachah* — which received two equally loud 'Amens' — and ate it. Then Gershon

Chapter Nine: Children / 115

was treated to a cookie, and this time Refael had the opportunity to join Reb Chaim in answering 'Amen.'

The boys left the store in high spirits. The gift Reb Chaim had given them was more than a mere couple of cookies — it was a memory which has endured for over forty years.

REB YESHAYA DAVIS RECOUNTED TO ME his days as a student at Yeshiva Torah Vodaath. He recalled all the efforts Reb Chaim made with the students to inculcate *brachos* into their daily lives. We already know how he distributed candy and knishes so that the children could make blessings and the others could answer "*Amen*."

"L'shem Shamayim, Kinderlach!"

But what, in particular, made an extreme impression on him was that when he and the other boys were playing ball in the street, Reb Chaim would urge them on with the following words: "*Kinderlach, l'shem Shamayim* — play your game for the sake of *Hashem*! When you play ball keep *Hashem* in mind. You play ball in order to keep healthy so that you may serve *Hashem*. Everything a Jew does must be for Heaven's sake, even routine and common practices like playing ball!"

Yeshaya Davis went on to say that this had a great influence on him. As he grew older and understood more, he realized that Reb Chaim's urging "*L'shem Shamayim, Kinderlach!*" had influenced his religious practices and his daily life a great deal.

AS REB CHAIM WAS ABLE TO INSTILL the love of *Yiddishkeit* and doing *mitzvos* in the yeshiva children, all the more did he do so with his own children. His life provided an example for his children and grandchildren to emulate.

Chinuch Habanim — Teaching of the Children

Reb Chaim disliked having to do anything that was not Torah or *mitzvah* related. He never read an English newspaper in his home; he felt it was a waste of time. Lurid headlines and accounts of undesirable events should not be read by adults, he believed, and should certainly be avoided by

*Reb Chaim, himself a twin, with twin great-grandchildren
Adinah and Galiah Fisher*

impressionable youngsters. He also had no interest in the popular radio stars of the day; the only time he turned on the radio was to listen to a Presidential address. Newspapers, radio and the like were but worldly time-killers. Reb Chaim's prime interests were *tzedakah*, *chessed*, and Torah.

His children respected him deeply, and when he entered a room they stood up for him without being prompted. They would also never contradict their parents, as prescribed by the *Shulchan Aruch*.

When Hena Gelb became ill and was unable to tend the store, her daughter Rose left school at the age of fifteen to take care of her mother and run the store. Even after the girls were grown and had found other employment, they awoke at 5 A.M. every Friday morning to help out in the store, as Friday was the busiest day and extra hands were always needed.

Tznius, modesty, was always emphasized in the Gelb household. Modest clothing that did not attract attention was the rule, following Yaakov *Avinu's* admonition to his children, *"Lama tisra'u* — Do not attract the attention of the people around you, causing envy."

Every *erev Shabbos* each child was assigned a specific task to perform in honor of the coming Sabbath. It is stressed in the Talmud, tractate *Kiddushin*, "*Mitzvah bo yoter mib'shalucho* — It is a bigger *mitzvah* if you perform it personally, rather than if you send someone to do it for you." The Talmud cites the examples of Rava, who salted fish himself, and Rav Safra, who burnt the hairs from the chicken himself to make it edible for Shabbos. Thus, everyone must personally do something to help prepare for Shabbos; proxies should not be used. Reb Chaim himself set a perfect example for his children, as he would remove all the dining-room furniture and get down on his hands and knees to wash the floor before Shabbos. In this manner he followed the example of the great rabbis quoted above, who placed their dignity aside when it came to the dignity and honor of Shabbos. He performed his tasks meticulously, and turned the simple chore into a masterpiece, doing it with flourish and enthusiasm.

The values Reb Chaim imparted to his children have stayed with them all their lives, and have been communicated in turn to his grandchildren and great-grandchildren, who are all living true Torah lives.

CHAPTER TEN
Teshuvah and Prayer

Reb Chaim's Prayer

PEOPLE WHO HAVE *DAVENED* with Reb Chaim and participated in a *minyan* at which he was present tell of a moving experience. When the *Kedushah* is recited during the repetition of the *Shemoneh Esrai*, one raises one's body as it is said, to follow the procedure of the angels as they say it. In his exuberance to emulate the angels, Reb Chaim would actually leap off the floor during his *davening*.

When he *davened* in the *shul* on the first floor of the yeshiva, students in the classrooms on the third floor could hear the resonance of his *Amens*. Tears rolled down his face in a stream as he pleaded to *Hashem* to answer his prayers and bestow upon *klal Yisrael* His abundant blessings and mercy. What was even more remarkable was that he did this three times every day. The prayers which many of us say each day are often recited by rote, with little attention paid to what is actually being said. Reb Chaim, however, was able to impart this heartfelt *kavanah* even to his everyday prayers. He was an inspiration to everyone who heard him.

REB CHAIM'S PRAYER had a powerful effect in an unexpected situation and an unlikely location. This story first came to my attention in an Anglo-Jewish newspaper in Connecticut. A congregation in that state had just completed the building of a

Chapter Ten: Teshuvah and Prayer / 119

The Purpose of a Shul

beautiful new *shul*. It was a magnificent edifice. The finest architects had been employed, and no money had been spared to achieve the salient beauty which this synagogue possessed. The finest artisans used the best available materials in its construction. The newspaper article related that a ceremony had been held to dedicate the new building. All the congregants gathered in their best finery for this auspicious occasion.

As the members entered the sanctuary, many approached the rabbi of the *shul* to engage him in conversation. The question most frequently posed to the rabbi was, "How much did this cost?" Other questions and comments were in the same vein. "Who was the architect?" "Where did the material come from?" "The seats are plusher than movie seats!"

The rabbi, who was well aware of the difficulties, time, energy, money, and effort expended to construct this edifice, was suddenly struck by a thought which penetrated his weary mind. *Was this what we had toiled so hard for? Was all the labor worth the final goal?* Judging from the remarks he had heard all day, the members of this *shul* had completely overlooked the purpose of this building. The rabbi recalled that when he had been a student in Yeshiva Torah Vodaath, a man named Reb Chaim Gelb had *davened* there. He remembered that the eloquence and feeling with which Reb Chaim had uttered the *Kaddish* prayer made one feel as if he were standing right in front of G-d Himself. And the manner in which he also urged the rest of the congregants to join him with the same intensity that he exuded, manifested the phrase "*Shivisi Hashem L'negdi Tamid* — I place G-d before me at all times."

Thinking about Reb Chaim, the rabbi realized what a *shul* should be. The humble surroundings in which Reb Chaim had prayed could not compare to the physical beauty of this new synagogue. But the rabbi, basking in the glow of this enormous achievement and at the pinnacle of his success, realized that all of this creation was vanity. Without the proper *kavanah*, feeling, this could not be a true *shul*.

The rabbi himself related this story in the newspaper. Reb

Chaim's *kavanah*, sincerity, and purity of heart had taught an inspiring lesson to a young rabbi many years later, in a place where Reb Chaim had never set foot. The true purpose of a *shul* — as a place to pray and communicate with *Hashem*, and not as a means of flaunting wealth — was brought home by the power of Reb Chaim's prayer.

Reb Chaim's Minchah

DURING THE PAST SEVERAL DECADES we have witnessed the phenomenal growth in the awareness of Torah and *Yiddishkeit* throughout this country. New yeshivos are springing up all over the United States. There has been a resurgence in the study of *daf yomi*, daily learning of a page of the Talmud.

Another development, especially prevalent in New York City, is the proliferation of *minyanim* for *Minchah* at various places of employment. Especially during the short days of winter, it is difficult to find the time or the place to *daven Minchah* at the proper hour. Nowadays, many *minyanim* have been established throughout the city.

When Reb Chaim was employed, however, these did not exist. People did not have the time to leave work and travel to a *shul* to *daven Minchah*. What did Reb Chaim do? He organized a *minyan* right in his place of business. Fortunately, his employers were thoughtful, considerate people and did not object to this. Every afternoon he went around gathering the workers to pray. Although everyone was busy, Reb Chaim always managed to find at least ten men who were willing to lay aside their work to form a *minyan*. He was thus able to *daven* with a *minyan* three times every day, while enabling others to do so as well.

The Key to Success

DAVE TRAUB, WHO HAD A DRY-GOODS STORE in Williamsburg, worked together with Reb Chaim Gelb at B.I.B. on Broadway in downtown Manhattan before he went into his own business. He relates that Reb Chaim was a superlative salesman whose bosses were continually amazed at his outstanding salesmanship. It is told that at one time they wired him to *stop* selling, as they were out of stock! Mr. Traub told me that the proprietors of B.I.B. sent two men to check on him and find out his mode of operating, in the hopes that they could teach his methods to the other salesmen.

Mr. Traub also stated that wherever he went, under any circumstances, Reb Chaim would never fail to find the time to *daven Minchah*. Even if he was in the store of a non-Jew, if he saw the sky beginning to darken, he would realize that it was time for *Minchah*. He was very careful about this, as the time for saying the afternoon prayers is limited; if the proper time passes, one can no longer fulfill the *mitzvah* that day. So if the time for *Minchah* fell during his working hours — even if he was in a non-Jewish establishment — Reb Chaim interrupted the negotiations and asked the proprietor where he could find a quiet spot for prayer, so that he might fulfill his religious obligations. He never was embarrassed or afraid to do so. He would stand in the designated location and pray slowly and with feeling. Instead of generating negative feelings, this practice gained him respect in the eyes of his customers.

Looking back, I am sure that the key to his success was his unwavering adherence to his religious principles. Reb Chaim's customers realized how, in effect, he put his job in jeopardy — and responded warmly to him. Many other religious people have since found that the observance of their religion was not a hindrance in their climb to success, but was rather a great aid to them.

A Call to Teshuvah

DURING THE MANY YEARS THAT REB CHAIM lived near the yeshiva, he kept in contact with all the students who passed through its portals. He continually exhorted the children to make the blessings and to answer *Amen*, as mentioned in a previous anecdote. His personality, his sincerity, and his *bren* (burning — of the flame of *Yiddishkeit*) had an impact on them which lasted for many years and influenced them much later in life.

A story was told to me of one of the former students of the yeshiva, who had moved far away into surroundings most

Reb Chaim leading the congregation in Tehillim

unconducive to Yiddishkeit. He strayed far from the teachings of his rabbis, as he was in an area devoid of observant Jews, and he fell into the pattern of his community.

One night, he had a dream in which Reb Chaim vividly appeared to him and called him by name. This appearance brought forth a flood of feelings in the dreamer, and reminded him of his yeshiva days spent learning Torah. He awoke with a start; the dream had been so lifelike that the experience evoked a shock wave of repentance. He did a complete turnabout and returned to his observant ways. He has remained religious to this day, and his children are now also attending yeshiva.

The Story of Yekusiel Zodok (Carl) Kagan

WHEN I STARTED TO WRITE THIS TRIBUTE to Reb Chaim at the behest of his daughter — my wife, Shirley — I had no idea where it would lead me. I have been amazed and sometimes overwhelmed by what people have told me. I have learned a lot about my father-in-law which I never knew. I am sure that there are countless other tales which have not yet come to my attention.

One of the most remarkable tributes to Reb Chaim was that of Mr. Yekusiel Zodok Kagan. I was sitting in my kitchen not long ago when the phone rang. I picked it up to find Yekusiel Kagan calling from Worcester, Massachusetts.

He was so emotional that he could barely talk, but the first words he uttered revealed a remarkable story. "Chaim Gelb saved my life spiritually," he said, and then started to tell a story that began about eighty years ago. Around the turn of the century his grandfather was sent by the *Chofetz Chaim* to Harbin, China to serve as a *shochet*, ritual slaughterer, or more precisely, *shochet-cum-rav* for the small Jewish community there. At the time, this community consisted of only eight families, but by the time he left in 1926 it had grown to about 3,000 members. Although it was a great sacrifice for him and his family, he undertook this assignment and remained in Harbin until the day that the son of a colleague cast away his Judaism by symbolically throwing his *tefillin* on the floor and spitting on them. When the elder Rabbi Kagan witnessed this occurrence, he realized that it was time to leave Harbin, as the community had come under the atheistic influence of the Soviet Union.

Yekusiel's father settled in Williamsburg and had five sons, all of whom studied in Yeshiva Torah Vodaath. Yekusiel's early recollections of Reb Chaim are from when, as youngsters, he and his friends would come to the yeshiva early to play ball in the schoolyard. Reb Chaim would herd them all into the *shul* so that they would hear *Kaddish* and answer, "Amen, Y'hai Shmai Rabbah," with the promise of a reward of a piece of candy or a penny or two. In that way the boys came to call him "the *Kaddish* man." He recalls with pride how he and his brother used to deliver *challos* for Reb Chaim to the Bostoner *Rebbe* and the Skolyer *Rebbe*, for which they received the magnificent remuneration of twenty-five cents.

Yekusiel later went to high school at Yeshiva Rabbi Jacob Joseph on the East Side of Manhattan, and also attended Yeshiva Be'er Shmuel under Rabbi Horowitz. But he got his *hashkafah* mostly from Reb Chaim Gelb.

"I learned *midos* from him," Yekusiel told me. "Just by watching him, one learned how to be kind. He was a walking fortress of *chessed*. One could learn to be a kind Jew, to love his fellow Jew, just by observing Reb Chaim's actions."

Yekusiel went on to say, "Although I was also influenced by many *rabbanim*, Reb Chaim was a layman and as such was so great. I loved him. All my life he has been in my mind. Wherever I went, I always thought of him. He saved my life spiritually. He kept me — his memory kept me — on the path of Torah." He then asked me to send him a picture of Reb Chaim for his grandson, who attends a yeshiva in New England. As is the current custom, his class has pictures of all the *gedolim* of the generation, and he wants to put Reb Chaim's picture in with them. "There is no one like him today," said Yekusiel Kagan. "He was special. His *frumkeit* and sincerity were unparalleled."

Mr. Kagan was so emotional and overcome merely by speaking

of his relationship with Reb Chaim that I did not want to intrude on his memories. I felt that it was improper for me to probe into his inner feelings, so I just let him talk and transcribed but a fragment of all he told me. When Yekusiel told me, "Reb Chaim saved my life spiritually because his memory and deeds were constantly in my mind," it was not an exaggeration but an actuality.

Yekusiel Kagan, you see, spent nine years in the United States Army, serving in Korea and in France. I do not have to relate at length all the tests a soldier undergoes trying to remain true to Torah and *Yiddishkeit*. Yekusiel was confronted every step of the way with challenges, tests and temptations, and only the constant thought of Reb Chaim kept him true to Torah. Even to this day, Reb Chaim is constantly on his mind.

His last recollection of Reb Chaim is that when he came to Williamsburg to visit his father, he took his father to the barber on Lee and Wilson Streets. Reb Chaim spotted him there, recognized him even after all these years, and ran to him, shouting, "Sweetie! Sweetie!" Such was the love that was manifested by him toward his fellow Jew.

CHAPTER ELEVEN
Midos — Character

Reb Chaim's Modesty and Humility

IF ONE DOES A GOOD DEED, one generally likes to bask in the enveloping afterglow of that good deed. Understandably, people like to relate to others the outstanding deeds that they have accomplished. However, Reb Chaim never bragged about the *mitzvos* he performed. Anonymity was the key to his *maasim tovim*. The person who received his assistance never needed to be concerned about being embarrassed about taking charity, because Reb Chaim never told anyone who his recipients were. Even when pressed to do so, he would never reveal a name; the most he would do was say that it was a *talmid chacham*, or a sick person, or something of that general nature.

Reb Chaim would never discuss any of his achievements. He neither expected nor wanted any acclaim or fanfare. Helping the needy person was sufficient reward for him.

He never asked for credit or *kavod*, honor, for any of the good deeds he performed. How, then, do we know of all the stories related in this book? People who participated or witnessed these many *mitzvos* have proudly come forward and told how he helped them. They were impressed by his modesty and humility, and proud to have been associated with him.

The Baal Chov

EVERYONE MUST BECOME A DEBTOR on some occasion in his life. If you purchase a car on the installment plan you slowly pay off the debt. When you buy a home, you obtain a mortgage which must be paid off over twenty or thirty years. Often, people must borrow money to arrange a wedding or a *bar-mitzvah* celebration for a child. Everyone has at one time or another been a debtor, a *baal chov*.

Reb Chaim had *chovos* of a different sort, which he mentioned to people when collecting funds for charity. "I am a *baal chov*," he would tell them, and everyone knew to which debts he was referring. He had debts to pay for charities to which he had obligated himself. He paid rent, medical bills, and the like for many indigent individuals.

Yes, Reb Chaim was a *baal chov*, a debtor. But he had no personal debts, for he never borrowed for his own meager personal needs. He was a perpetual debtor for charity.

❦ ❦ ❦

Rabbi Moshe Rivlin was the well-known financial director of Yeshiva Torah Vodaath. He was a creative and innovative person. He realized that the average person could not afford a large donation to the yeshiva. Therefore, he arranged a cooperative program with several free-loan societies, whereby the societies would lend sums of money to these individuals who would repay the loan in affordable monthly payments. The yeshiva would benefit immediately, however, as the money would go directly to it.

Refael Shain was approached by Rabbi Rivlin for such a loan and was told by him, "I want you to know that Reb Chaim Gelb takes out large loans for the Yeshiva, making the payments from the money he collects and from his own personal funds. He donates huge sums in this manner, not only to Torah Vodaath but to many other yeshivos as well. He is one of the staunchest supporters of Torah we have." These were the debts to which Reb Chaim referred when he told his donors that he was a *baal chov*.

Reb Chaim's House

REB CHAIM LIVED IN A FOUR-STORY BROWNSTONE in Williamsburg, the same house in which his parents had lived. After his parents' passing he purchased this home from the estate, and it became his castle until his wife Hena passed away.

Many stories have been related here in which Reb Chaim's home played a major role and figured in important incidents in his life. The house served as a place for people to gather on Shabbos, for a place to sleep or receive a meal. Our rabbis tell us that Avraham *Avinu* planted an *aishel*, which is variously interpreted as either a wayfarers' inn or a tree under which he served his guests. Whoever wished to enter his home would receive sustenance and aid, as the Torah teaches us. Reb Chaim's household was conducted in the same fashion; his home was open to all. To him, the home was another tool with which to serve *Hashem*, to do *mitzvos*, and to help others.

Today in the Jewish community there are many beautiful, fashionable and expensive houses. However, Reb Chaim looked upon his beautiful home not as a materialistic achievement, but rather as a vehicle to do *mitzvos* and serve *Hashem*, and nothing more.

After his wife's death the house became too large for him to cope with. He ruminated for quite a while on the proper method of disposing of this lovely home. His first thoughts were to convert it into a *mikveh*, following his philosophy that his home should be used for holy purposes only. His attempts in this direction were unsuccessful. Finally, he decided to donate it to a yeshiva for a fraction of its true value. His life's priorities were such that money never played a role in his decision-making. The factor that counted most was the spiritual aspect of the venture into which he was about to enter. He was happy without the material aspects of life. He didn't need a luxurious home to give him satisfaction; he would be happy living anywhere, as long as he was able to pursue his Torah way of life.

This attribute was manifested after he sold his house to the yeshiva. He then moved into a single room, where his furnishings

Chapter Eleven: Midos — Character / 129

consisted of a bed, a bureau and a table and chairs. When our family told him that we wished to refurbish his room with new furniture, he strongly forbade us to do so. Yet even under these impoverished circumstances he always remained in a happy frame of mind.

Kashrus

IN THE FIRST HALF OF THIS CENTURY not many food items were under proper rabbinical supervision, as they are today. At the present time, when one enters the supermarket one is confronted with innumerable items under Orthodox *hashgachah*: canned goods, candies, drinks, bread, snacks, ice cream, and so on. However, when Reb Chaim was younger, the situation was completely reversed; there was a tremendous scarcity of properly supervised kosher products.

Reb Chaim, therefore, instituted in his home the rule that everything must be home made; he and his family would thus not have to rely on products of dubious *kashrus*. Only fresh fruits and vegetables were used, and these were meticulously checked by Hena Gelb for bugs and worms. Even when the number of reliable kosher products began to increase, Reb Chaim stuck to his rule and refused to buy any of these products. All dairy products he used were *cholov Yisrael*, and he never allowed any meats in his house that had been prepared outside. When a scandal arose at one time, which cast a dark cloud on items that had been accepted by the Orthodox community as kosher, Reb Chaim and his family were not affected by this because of his practice of never buying any of these items.

Reb Chaim avoided eating outside his own home. When he went to a wedding or other *simchah* he always brought along his own small package of food that had been prepared at home. He did this surreptitiously, however, as he did not wish to cast aspersions on the *kashrus* of the establishment, which did bear a reliable *hechsher*. It was just Reb Chaim's way not to eat any food that had not been prepared in his own home.

Significant changes have taken place in the field of *kashrus* over the past several decades. Many, if not most, of today's housewives have never had the experience of *kashering* meat or poultry. Today this process is performed by the butcher. Although *kashering* is generally taught in most girls' yeshivos in order that this *mitzvah* might not be forgotten, it is rarely practiced inside the home. Many years ago, however, the Jewish housewife had to go to the live market and wait for the *shochet*, the ritual slaughterer, to slaughter the chicken. Then the woman would take it home, pluck and *kasher* it.

Needless to say, Hena Gelb was always present at the ritual slaughter of the chickens she would buy, and was meticulous in her *kashering* process at home. On numerous occasions she would notice a bruise or break on the wing or leg of a chicken, which necessitated an immediate consultation with an Orthodox rabbi to see if the animal was still kosher. She was cautious about the slightest possible imperfection or abnormality, and would always check it out with a competent authority.

It is no wonder, in light of the stringent standards of the Gelb kitchen, that the greatest of *rebbeim* unhesitatingly ate in Reb Chaim's home.

The Satmar Rebbe's Recommendation

IT IS TOLD THAT A JEWISH PERSON in need of a solution to a pressing problem visited the Satmar *Rebbe*, z"l, to receive his blessing. After this individual related his problem to the *Rebbe*, who was known as a great *tzaddik* and scholar, the *Rebbe* bestowed his blessing upon the supplicant. Before the man left, the *Rebbe* volunteered this bit of information to him, "It is better to receive a blessing from two people, rather than from one person."

The man inquired, "Whom should I visit for the second blessing?"

"Go to Reb Chaim Gelb," replied the *Rebbe*.

Chapter Eleven: Midos — Character / 131

Rabbi Yaakov Kaminetsky Recites a Blessing

RABBI YAAKOV KAMINETSKY was one of the leading *roshei yeshiva* of the past generation. Among his children are Rabbi Shmuel Kaminetsky, founder and *rosh yeshiva* of the Philadelphia Yeshiva, and Rabbi Binyamin Kaminetsky, founder and *rosh yeshiva* of the Yeshiva of South Shore.

In his role as *rosh yeshiva*, Rabbi Yaakov Kaminetsky was invited to participate in and perform many weddings of students. He frequently met Reb Chaim, who attended these weddings to collect money for his many causes, and the two men became well acquainted. There was a period of time when Rabbi Kaminetsky did not meet Reb Chaim for quite a while. Rabbi Kaminetsky expressed his concern and wondered whether Reb Chaim was all right. Finally, after a year during which their paths did not converge, they did meet again at a wedding. Reb Yeshaya Davis related that when Rabbi Kaminetsky spotted Reb Chaim, he went over to Reb Chaim and embraced him warmly. In addition, he recited the blessing "Mechayeh Hameisim" (Reviver of the Dead), which is recited upon seeing a loved one following an absence of a year.

The Bostoner Rebbe Visits Reb Chaim

MRS. GOLDMAN WAS PUTTERING ABOUT in her kitchen, preparing dinner. She went over to the stove to check on the cooking, when she was interrupted by the ringing of the telephone. She picked up the receiver and heard, "Long distance calling for Mr. Chaim Gelb." She almost dropped the phone in her excitement. Long distance — it must be urgent! She ran into the hall and called, "Hena, Hena — quick, long distance for Reb Chaim!" There was a current of excitement in the air. In those days when few people had telephones, long-distance calls were made only in cases of extreme importance. The Gelbs had no phone, but Mrs. Goldman, their tenant, did, and was kind enough to call them when they received a call on her telephone. She had given the Gelbs permission to give her number to people who wanted to call the Gelbs. Reb Chaim bounded up the stairs two at a time and quickly picked up the phone. He was very surprised when he heard the voice of the Bostoner *Rebbe* on the other end. The *Rebbe* told him that he was coming to New York and would like to stay with the Gelbs. The *Rebbe* had heard of Chaim Gelb, and when he had to come to New York, he decided that this was the man with whom he wished to stay, a man who would make him feel as though he were in his own home. He was to visit them for six weeks.

How would they house the *Rebbe* and his family? The girls would stay with friends and the *Rebbe* would thus be able to reside in the front portion of the house. It was an ideal arrangement for the *Rebbe*, and Reb Chaim and his family were happy to serve the *Rebbe* and his family. It was a historic occasion for them, and a tremendous opportunity for showing the children how one must perform the *mitzvah* of *hachnasas orchim*, welcoming guests. Hena Gelb did the cooking for all. Every morning Avigdor, Reb Chaim's son, got up very early to go with a new, glass container that had been immersed in a *mikveh* to Balsam's farm in East New York to bring milk for the *Rebbe* so he could have *cholov Yisrael*. [Although it is halachically permissible to buy milk that is sold in an unimmersed glass container, for his personal use the *Rebbe* would not eat any food that had been prepared or stored in unimmersed containers.] Hena would pasteurize the milk and make cheese and butter from it.

For six weeks the Gelb home was flooded by throngs of people from all walks of life who came to receive the *Rebbe's* blessings, prayers and advice. People who needed *parnassah*, people who were childless, those who were about to start a business, — all sought his advice and blessings. The sick and lame came to Rabbi Pinchas Horowitz to ask him to pray for them.

Meanwhile, Reb Chaim and Hena catered to the *Rebbe's* every need so that he would be able to give his full attention to the needy who flocked to him for help and succor. They never expected any reward; on the contrary, the very fact that the *Rebbe* honored them with his presence was reward in itself. The *mitzvah* was its own reward, and they made the *Rebbe* feel at home.

ONE OF THE PREVALENT EVILS IN OUR SOCIETY is the sin of *lashon hara*, speaking evil of another person. Even in the time of the Talmud, many people engaged in *avak lashon hara*, which is defined as not really speaking evil but rather hinting at *lashon hara*. The question arises: Why do people engage in this activity? There are many reasons given, but the most common one is jealousy or envy. Our Rabbis tell us that one really does not derive pleasure from *lashon hara*, just as a snake does not get pleasure from biting someone. Yet this activity is constantly among us.

Avoiding Lashon Hara

How can we solve this problem? Reb Chaim showed us a way. Those who knew him and were close to him can testify that they never heard him speak *lashon hara*. It was as foreign to him as eating unkosher food.

Reb Chaim was totally immersed in the performance of *mitzvos*. He was so busy running around collecting for his various charities, *davening*, doing acts of *chessed*, and performing his myriad other Torah-related activities that he never had time to waste in speaking *lashon hara*. He never had the time to engage in idle conversation, which often leads to the commission of this sin. From Reb Chaim we can learn that if we set our priorities correctly, we would not have time for *lashon hara*.

BEFORE THE HOLIDAY OF PASSOVER, Jewish law states, one must sell all the *chametz*, leaven, in his possession. Usually one goes to the rabbi of the congregation with which he is affiliated, and the rabbi then acts as a *shaliach*, agent, in transferring the *chametz* into the possession of a non-Jew. In this way one thereby fulfills the injunction of not owning *chametz* for the duration of the Passover holiday. It is necessary to perform this *mitzvah* only one time each year; however, Reb Chaim found an opportunity within the performance of this *mitzvah* to be *mehaneh talmidei chachamim* (to be beneficial to Torah scholars). It is customary at the time of the performance of this *mitzvah* to bestow a sum of money on the individual who acts as one's agent. So on *erev Pesach*, Reb Chaim

Mechiras Chametz

made the rounds. He visited every rabbi and *rebbe* in Williamsburg and the Lower East Side of Manhattan to perform this mitzvah, thus benefiting them all.

THE FOLLOWING INCIDENT WAS RELATED to me by Reb Shiya Wilhelm.

Bris Milah When his son Shmuel Baruch was born, the *bris* had to be performed in the hospital. In those days, more than forty years ago, women routinely stayed in the hospital for ten days after giving birth; thus a *bris*, which must be performed on the eighth day, was frequently done in the hospital.

A problem arose in connection with the hospital *bris*: How could the *mitzvah* of *metzitza b'peh* (a portion of the circumcision ritual frowned upon by some physicians) be performed in this hospital which was against such a practice? Reb Shiya tried to make arrangements with a doctor to permit the *metzitza b'peh*; however, his plea failed. When the day of the *bris* arrived, the *mohel* was instructed to fulfill the *mitzvah* properly. However, the hospital had posted a nurse in the room to prevent this procedure. When the moment of the circumcision arrived, a remark was made to the effect that the *mohel* should not do it. Reb Chaim, who overheard this remark, quickly began to shout, "America is a country of freedom! No one can curtail my freedom to practice my religion as I wish. America is a free country!" All the others joined in this chant. The nurse fled in panic, and the *bris* was performed with *metzitza b'peh*, according to *halachah*.

REB CHAIM GELB LIVED ON DIVISION AVENUE in Williamsburg, Brooklyn. On the next block there was an institution that played a

Mikveh — The Ritual Bath major role in his life, the *mikveh*, or ritual bath, located on the first floor of the *Polisher shtiebl* (the synagogue frequented by Polish Jews). The *mikveh* was under their auspices, and all the religious men and women of Williamsburg utilized it.

Reb Chaim immersed himself in the *mikveh* every day of the

week, including Shabbos. No matter what the weather conditions, no matter what the state of his health, nothing could deter Reb Chaim from the daily performance of this *mitzvah*. Even if the snow was piled several feet high in front of his door, Reb Chaim would manage to wend his way there every morning so that he could then recite his prayers in a state of *kedushah*, sanctity. Many less-hardy souls found a *heter*, dispensation, in bad weather, in that it was a life-threatening situation to immerse oneself in the *mikveh* in such inclement weather.

Reb Chaim, however, did not avail himself of any excuses. He felt that no harm could befall him in the performance of a *mitzvah*; he would quote our Rabbis' promise, "*Shiluchei mitzvah aynam nizakim* — people performing a *mitzvah* cannot be harmed." The fact was that in all the years that he performed this *mitzvah* daily, not once did he become ill from it. In addition, many times when he was actually sick, no amount of persuasion or coaxing could make him refrain from going. In fact, he even claimed that it made him feel better!

Many times Reb Chaim was invited to another neighborhood for Shabbos, to participate in a *bar-mitzvah* celebration or other *simchah*. Before he would accept the invitation, he would always ask, "Is there a *mikveh* within walking distance?" If there wasn't, he would not attend the function, no matter how important the person making the affair. His daily ritual would not be compromised for anyone or for any occasion. The people whose invitations he refused did not feel slighted or insulted, however. They understood and respected his convictions and acknowledged his deep faith in all religious matters.

This ritual of daily immersion in the *mikveh* is but a microcosm of Reb Chaim's philosophy of life. Hardly anyone could match his tenacity and perseverance in attempting to perform all 613 *mitzvos*. This was but one manifestation of his steadfastness in Torah observance.

Reb Chaim dancing at a simchah

WE LIVE IN A CHANGING SOCIETY, and many of the changes being wrought are detrimental to the community, especially the Jewish community. One plague that is becoming more prevalent now is the trend of broken marriages. In American society as a whole, almost half of all marriages end in divorce. Although the divorce rate among Orthodox Jews is much lower, it has also been on the rise in recent years.

Marriages Are Forever

Even couples with many children are not immune. Can you imagine the spiritual and psychological damage inflicted upon the children of these broken marriages? An observant home ideally should have both parents present to be most proficient in the job of raising children to be Torah-true Jews. The concept of honoring one's father and mother, which is interwoven into the fabric of our faith, cannot be taught properly if there is an ongoing conflict between the parents. The list of consequences is long.

Reb Chaim Gelb was very perspicacious in this matter. Fifty years ago, whoever attended a wedding at which Reb Chaim was present bore witness to an occurrence that was strange but significant, especially when viewed from today's perspective. After the wedding ceremony, culminating in the traditional breaking of the glass, a short man would be seen getting up on a chair, the better to make himself heard. He would proclaim in a loud voice which was audible above the din of the hundreds of assembled guests, "A contract for 120 years!" implying that this marriage, as all marriages should, will last forever.

Although the decorum of the festivities had been interrupted, everyone would shout "*Amen!*" in agreement. Reb Chaim, in that one sentence, wanted to insure the future of our people. That could be accomplished only through a solid, strong and enduring family life. He summed up that concept so magnificently and succinctly that it is hard to match. A contract for 120 years. Marriage is forever.

Anything for Shalom Bayis

THE FOLLOWING INCIDENT OCCURRED during the Great Depression, and portrays how financial distress could contribute to the deterioration of *shalom bayis*.

In the Depression years, even professionals were hard hit. In many fields it was difficult to earn enough to attain financial security or support a family. Many educated people were forced to leave their chosen professions and accept whatever menial labor they could find. Many professionals obtained factory jobs to survive.

Jack was a lawyer who somehow managed to remain in his chosen field even in those dark days. He was not as successful as he had hoped to be, however. Coming home from work was no longer a pleasant experience. He recalled the early days of his marriage and remembered the happiness he had felt, looking forward to a long, pleasant life with his wife. He remembered his feelings of expectation and ambition, his conviction that the world would be his. He had been confident in his ability, and felt that he would set the world on fire. He recalled the great pride that had enveloped him when he first hung out his shingle, proclaiming to everyone that Jack Cohen (not his real name) was prepared to offer his legal services to all who needed them. At that time he was convinced that he would practice law in such a way that people from all over the world would make their way to his door, clamoring for his assistance.

Now, though, he dreaded returning home after a day's work in the office. He could vividly picture the scene that would confront him when he walked through the door. The first question would be, "Did you have any clients today?" His answer would again be negative, and then the downhill slide would begin. His wife would look at him in disappointment, as if he had intentionally let her down. Clients were hard to come by; didn't she know that? When a client would appear, it was always for some insignificant, unchallenging task that would yield but a paltry fee. In some months he barely earned enough to pay his rent; that was the worst of all, because he was then forced to ask his father-in-law for a loan to cover the deficit. This was abhorrent to his nature, and he also knew what his wife had to endure when requesting help from her parents.

After he informed his wife about his continuing lack of success, the air in his home would become charged. At first she would comfort him and tell him not to worry, things were soon bound to change for the better. Everyone found it difficult to get started, she would say, but eventually he would do well. In the first year of their marriage they were still happy and hopeful; their wedding presents took up some of the slack in income, and their requirements were few.

But then things subtly began to change. He noticed changes coming over his wife when he told her of his failures. No longer was she the encouraging soul, but she had become morose and bitter, though still falling short of direct accusations. She was not the same sweet girl he had married, but had become nervous and restless as she felt more deprived and denied. He tried his best to make her happy and cheerful, but he could still discern her underlying disappointment and unhappiness.

It gnawed silently at his insides that he was not able to support his wife in the manner which he would have liked. When he entered his home now, silence reigned after an exchange of perfunctory greetings. Every insignificant item took on major proportions. Now they feared to talk to each other.

Things had briefly changed for the better after the birth of their first child, a boy, whom they both adored. His wife had perked up and happiness again seemed to reign. But with another mouth to feed, Jack had to try harder than ever to succeed in his business, and his endeavors continued to be futile. He contacted various people and organizations in search of clients. He spent time visiting people he thought could help him. He put in longer hours. He called his old classmates from law school, but they were doing no better than he. After five or six years of marriage, he was still on the bottom rung of the ladder of success.

One day Jack's wife, Nancy, came into Hena Gelb's store. Hena, who had known Nancy since childhood, knew that Jack was struggling in his career, but had no inkling of their marital strife. She greeted Nancy cheerfully. "Hello, Nancy, how are you and how is Jack?"

"Fine, thank you," Nancy responded automatically. "I would like to speak to you privately, when you have the time."

Hena did not find this request particularly unusual, since many people often sought her out for advice. She told Nancy, "I'll be finished here shortly. Then I'll close the store and we'll go into the house, and talk over a cup of tea."

Nancy agreed to this, and waited in the store while Hena served her remaining customers. When the last customer had departed, Hena hung a sign in her window stating that the store was closed, but that she could be reached at home if needed. She took Nancy's arm and they went home together. Hena prepared tea and cake for the two of them, and they sat down at the table.

Hena had been prepared for a friendly chat, and was shocked by the first words that Nancy uttered. "Hena," she cried, "I want a divorce!"

Hena could not believe her ears. She had thought Jack and Nancy's relationship to be an idyllic one, and could not believe that Nancy would want to break it apart.

"Divorce!" she repeated. "Divorce? You're joking, aren't you? You and Jack are two wonderful people. He has a good profession, and I'm sure that he will soon be able to provide for you as your heart desires."

Suddenly Nancy burst out in a flood of uncontrollable tears, as the pent-up emotions of the last few frustrating years spilled out. She told Hena that because of the lack of money they had drifted apart, and the marriage was now seriously foundering. She spoke of her great unhappiness, which was in no small measure due to their lack of financial security. She had few clothes, they had not had a vacation in years. She recited a litany of lacks and woes.

Hena was shocked. What could she do? She consoled Nancy to the best of her ability, and told her that things were bound to become better. Nancy did not seem able to accept Hena's words, and her tears did not subside.

Hena was perplexed and heartbroken. Not only were her friends miserable, but what of their little boy? How could he grow up in a home without a father? She appealed to Nancy, but it seemed to be of no use. "Jack is such a fine man, an excellent husband and father. Give him more time. It will pay off, trust me," she pleaded.

But the bottom line was that there was no money in the house. Nancy was tired of the deprivation she and her child had suffered for so many years. She wanted out.

Hena asked her, "Does Jack know of your plans?"

"No," replied Nancy. "That's why I came to you first. I wanted to open my heart to you. I felt that if you could convince me to stay with him, I would be happy to listen. I have heard everything you have told me, but I still feel strongly that if the financial problem isn't solved, everything will be useless. This I will admit to you, Hena: If there were a solution to our economic situation, I would give the marriage another try, but as long as there is a dearth of money, the outlook is bleak."

Hena then said to her, "Do me a personal favor. Don't tell Jack anything yet. Give me a chance to mull this over. Come back in a few days and we'll discuss it again."

"Well," said Nancy, "out of respect for you I will do so, but it still seems hopeless."

Nancy left Hena pacing back and forth in her home, wondering how she could help her friends out of their predicament. That night Hena told Reb Chaim about the Cohens' problem, and he too was shocked.

Hena had her dinner, then sat down to think. Suddenly she was seized with an idea which might work, although it was a drastic notion. *Nancy is desperate*, thought Hena, *so I must make it work*.

The day came when Nancy returned to Hena's home. Hena reiterated many of the things she had already pointed out, and reemphasized the fineness and outstanding qualities of Nancy's husband. She pointed out that it would be foolish to leave such a fine man and cause additional devastation and hardship for the family. Finally they both were quiet, and sat staring at each other.

Hena then spoke, quietly but strongly. "Nancy," she said, "I want you to take a job. You go to work and make money; then you won't feel so deprived. Just wait and see. Jack will be successful soon. With the addition of your income, you will have enough money to live well. You will be out of your rut."

Nancy looked at Hena in open-mouthed astonishment. She had never expected such an answer! In those days very few women worked outside the home. And there was the seemingly overwhelming problem of finding someone to care for her young child while she was at work. They certainly could not afford to pay someone to do so! But before she could frame this question, Hena said to her, as if reading her mind, "Don't worry about your son. I will take care of him here. Drop him off before you go to work, and you can be assured that he will be in good hands all day."

When the impact of Hena's offer finally hit home, Nancy was overwhelmed and burst into tears of gratitude. She agreed to try out Hena's plan.

Hena's suggestion, quite outlandish for that time, did in fact work. Nancy found a job, began to earn some money, and the marriage was saved. As the Depression began to lift, Jack became a highly successful lawyer and he and Nancy raised their family without any further problems. Years later Nancy told Hena how grateful she was for what Hena had done for her in her time of hardship, and how lucky she had been for listening to Hena's advice.

Preventing a Mistake

OFTEN WE BECOME SO INVOLVED in our own problems — so enmeshed and mired down — that we can no longer see anything clearly, not even a possible solution. At such times it takes another understanding, caring soul to help one out of this mire. The following incident will show how Hena Gelb, because of her deep concern, was able to help another young couple build a future and have a happy family life.

❈ ❈ ❈

During the hot summer months Hena would rise early to bake her famous chocolate cake, thus insuring that she would have an ample supply of this delicacy to satisfy all her customers. In the early morning it was cooler, and it was not so taxing to spend those hours by the hot oven. On this particular day she had already finished baking several cakes when the doorbell rang.

All the regular customers of the Gelbs' bakery knew that if the store was closed they could ring the bell at their home, which was just across the street, and receive prompt and courteous service. But it was not even seven o'clock yet, too early for a customer. The ringing was insistent, with an air of urgency about it. Who could be calling so early — and why?

Hena quickly ran to open the door. There stood a young woman with tears streaming down her face. Hena recognized her as her neighbor Paula (not her real name), with whom she had become quite friendly.

Paula, who was in her late twenties, had been seeing a nice young man for about eight years. This was not unusual in the Depression days, as many couples could not afford to get married. Salaries were low, and it was hard enough to support a single person, much less a family, on these subsistence wages. Many people had to support parents and siblings as well, and if they married, the rest of their family would be left in dire financial straits. Therefore, many weddings had to be postponed until more propitious times arrived and the young couple could finally walk unencumbered to the *chuppah*. Paula's was one of these cases.

This morning, Paula came rushing into Hena's house, sobbing violently and incoherently. After a long time Hena was able to soothe and calm her down enough to inquire as to the problem. "What is wrong?" she asked gently. "Tell me all about it. I'm sure it can't be as bad as it appears to you."

Through her tears Paula blurted, "David and I have decided to break up."

"Are you out of your mind? After going together for so many years, why have you decided to break up? I know the love you have for each other, and you are both religious and of good character — it is an excellent match! You will never find another man like David, and he will never find another woman like you. You make a perfect couple! What could possibly have happened that could cause you to make such a decision? I just can't believe it!"

Paula replied, "Precisely because all you say is true, because David is so fine and *frum* and I realize that this *shidduch* is one in a million — precisely because of this we decided to break up."

Hena looked at Paula uncomprehendingly, waiting for her to clarify her answer.

"You see," said Paula, "because of those reasons we are suffering so greatly. Because of the fact that we can't get married, life has become unbearable. I am so miserable and so is David, so we decided that it is better to break up and forget each other. If we don't see one another, then maybe we will be happy."

"Such foolishness!" cried Hena. "You are cutting off your nose to spite your face! Just the opposite will occur if you take such action. I know you both too well; you will be even more miserable if you don't see each other any more!

"Bring David here tomorrow, and we will discuss the matter further. I want you both here tomorrow evening at eight o'clock."

Paula replied, "All right, I'll get David to come."

Hena gave Paula breakfast and then both women went to work, with the faint but distant hope that maybe Hena would be able to come up with some ideas.

All day long Hena thought about the problem at hand. She found it difficult to concentrate on her work. She was deeply concerned and distressed by Paula's plight, which seemed to have no apparent solution. Her brow became furrowed with the constant question plaguing her: What will happen to Paula and David? What a lovely couple they were! They could have a happy, fulfilled life and produce a wonderful generation of children if only they had the chance!

When Reb Chaim returned home from his rounds that evening he noticed that Hena was preoccupied with something. After the children had gone to bed and the last dinner guest had left, he questioned the dramatic change in her mood. She told him about the dilemma confronting Paula and David. Reb Chaim immediately fell into a similar frame of mind, as he too began to think about the problem.

Hena slept fitfully that night. At about three o'clock in the morning she awoke with a start. A thought had just crossed her mind. "No," she thought, "it will be too hard. It will cost too much money." She thought about it some more, and then woke up Reb Chaim, exclaiming, "Chaim, *we* can make the wedding!"

Reb Chaim drowsily replied, "What wedding? Who's getting married?"

"Chaim, wake up! I'm talking about Paula and David!"

"You mean make a complete wedding?" inquired Reb Chaim. "In a hall?" Even Reb Chaim, who was so generous of spirit, looked at her incredulously.

"No, Chaim, that's not necessary," replied Hena. "We'll make it right here, in our living room. We'll invite just the immediate families on both sides. Chaim, we must do it now, or the *shidduch* will dissolve. We must not let that happen!"

Reb Chaim said, "If you say so, I agree."

"There is one more hurdle to cross," noted Hena. "We must get the bride and groom to agree to this. Tomorrow I am meeting with both of them, and I'll try my hardest to convince them."

All through the next day, Hena was sitting on pins and needles. How would Paula and David feel about this plan? Would they accept her offer? She prayed to *Hashem* all day that they would.

Finally the appointed hour arrived, and Hena greeted Paula and David at her door. "Welcome, come in," she said to them with a smile. They made small talk over tea and cake, until finally Hena interrupted the conversation with her announcement. "It's settled," she said sternly, "the two of you are getting married. Set the date for the first available opportunity."

"Wedding?" they exclaimed in unison. "You know we don't have the money for a wedding!"

Hena informed them, "I am making the wedding for you right here in this house. You will get married as soon as possible. I am doing this to avert a tragic mistake. You two want to break up? No! I interpret this as a sign from Heaven that you must get married right away! No more waiting — eight years is enough! It is destined for you to get married now. All your seemingly insurmountable problems will disappear. Listen to me!"

Hena began to talk, outlining her plans. The couple was too surprised by this unexpected turn of events to refuse, and they both suddenly realized that Hena had been right. It was destined for them to finally marry. Eight years of waiting had totally drained them, but they finally realized that this was the right path to take. Matters had been brought to a head at last, and they were forced to take action. They realized that they cared too much for each other to ever be apart.

They joyfully agreed to Hena's plan, and the arrangements were made. A rabbi was engaged to officiate, the guests were invited, and Hena prepared the food. Everyone involved realized that this was the correct course of action, and *Hashem* would surely help the newlyweds begin their long-delayed life together.

The night of the wedding arrived, and the home of Chaim Gelb was filled with the clamor and noise of the *simchah*. Everyone was decked out in their finery. The *kallah* was radiant, the *chassan* handsome. Toasts were made, and cries of "*Mazal·tov!*" resounded. The ceremony was performed with dignity, and when the groom was escorted to the *chuppah* by his blind father, everyone's eyes were filled with tears.

Needless to say, Paula and David are now living a fine, *frum* life with a wonderful family, thanks to the efforts of Hena and Chaim Gelb.

Mashiach as a Marriage Performer

RABBI BILLY HERSHKOWITZ'S WIFE was riding in a car with Reb Chaim, who was an old and dear friend of the family, when she told him that her son Shloime had just become a *chassan*. Reb Chaim's immediate response was, "*Mashiach* should be the *mesader kiddushin*" (the one who performs the wedding ceremony). Those who heard this spontaneous remark were so overcome by this *tefillah* and by its sincerity that they were speechless for several moments. Who could visualize a scene such as the one Reb Chaim had just depicted? The *chassan* and *kallah*, their dear children, being married by *Mashiach* himself! Such an idea could only originate in the mind of Reb Chaim!

A Prophetic Viewpoint

RABBI CHAIM FEIFER WAS ATTENDING a *melaveh malkah* at a friend's home. The conversation was about the proliferation of yeshivos, *shuls*, and so on. Rabbi Feifer called the attention of the guests to what he had heard from Reb Chaim many years earlier. Reb Chaim had said, "On every block a yeshiva, a *Bais Yaakov*, a *mikveh* and a *shtiebl* — then *Mashiach* will come!"

How prophetic these words seem today, as we watch the rapid spread of all these institutions. Indeed, there *are* many locations today in which Reb Chaim's dream block exists, with a yeshiva, a *Bais Yaakov*, a *mikveh* and a *shtiebl* on it.

Reb Chaim's Purim

THE *SHULCHAN ARUCH* TELLS US that the *halachah* for *Purim* day is that one should *daven Minchah* in the afternoon, and following that, one should partake of the *mitzvah* of *seudas Purim*. This *seudah*, or festive meal, is a great celebration of the occasion of *klal Yisrael* being saved from physical extinction at the fiendish hands of Haman and his henchmen. This was not a plot to extirpate our religious faith, as occurred in the story of Chanukah; rather, this was a threat of physical destruction and we thus celebrate our redemption from this threat in a physical manner by rejoicing with a festive meal.

During the day of *Purim* itself, there was a constant parade of people in Reb Chaim's house collecting charity, in fulfillment of the *mitzvah* of *matanos la'evyonim*, gifts to the poor, which is especially incumbent upon everyone on *Purim*. Throngs of well-wishers came and went all day long, bearing and receiving gifts of food, fulfilling the *mitzvah* of *mishloach manos* (sending portions of food to one's friends), and thus promoting friendship, a major aim of *Purim*. The dining-room table was decked out in its Sabbath finery, laden with all the delicacies that the capable Hena Gelb could produce. It was a joyous time, and good fellowship prevailed. Many visitors were prevailed upon to remain for the *Purim seudah*.

The *Purim seudah* often lasts for an extended period of time, long beyond the time for *Maariv* services to begin. Many of us are so carried away with the spirit of *Purim* that we fail to go to *shul* that night, and end up *davening* at home without a *minyan*, if at all.

Reb Chaim's home, on the other hand, was a gathering place for worshipers on the night that *Purim* ended. Reb Chaim set up a special *minyan* in his home for all the Jews who had neglected to attend the services in *shul*. At the conclusion of the holiday of *Purim*, people came from all over Williamsburg to participate in Reb Chaim's *minyan*. His home was filled to capacity and he welcomed all visitors graciously, his face wreathed in a broad smile for having the *zechus* of hosting this *minyan*. When the congregation assembled in his home uttered the *Shema* in unison, proclaiming the unity of *Hashem*, his heart was filled to overflowing with gratitude at his good fortune in being able to host this crowd. After the services, people returned home in an elevated mood, happy for having been able to participate in this *mitzvah*.

Civic Pride

REB CHAIM ALWAYS FELT GRATITUDE toward this country. Although he was only a youth of eight when he arrived here, he knew how hard the Jews had struggled in the old country to simply survive. Even as a child he had already felt the ancient hatred manifested towards the Jews there. He therefore was extremely thankful that these evil attitudes were not prevalent in America. He was grateful as well for the plethora of opportunities one had here to advance oneself, and for the religious freedom inherent in American society.

The democratic government — government of the people, by the people, and for the people — helped the Jews educationally and socially. It was for this reason that Reb Chaim always treated public servants, such as police officers and firefighters, with great respect. Whenever Reb Chaim met an officer of the law, he would greet him warmly, compliment him on the fine job he was doing, and thank him for the invaluable service he was performing for the public. He would go out of his way to treat public servants with respect and dignity. The police in his precinct knew him well, and liked and respected him.

The story is told of one night in the middle of winter, when there was a fire around the corner from Reb Chaim's house. It was bitter cold when the firemen came to extinguish the blaze. Reb Chaim, hearing the disturbance, arose, got dressed, and went outside to offer his aid. When he saw the firemen battling the freezing temperatures as well as the fire, he ran back home and prepared gallons of hot coffee for them, and returned to the scene to distribute cups to all of the weary firefighters, who could not thank him enough for his thoughtfulness.

A young boy named Whitman was a witness to that fire and to

Reb Chaim's kindness to the firefighters. Years later he became the owner of a large catering hall, and it was his policy not to allow charity collectors to "disturb" guests during an affair. He made one exception, however — Reb Chaim Gelb. When asked why, he would tell the story of the fire. "I saw that man's good heart. My door is always open to him."

In this manner did Reb Chaim perform a *kiddush Hashem*, bringing respect for our people from those who, representing the secular government, performed important services for us.

Facing the Judge

WHEN THE FIRST SETTLERS, the Puritans and Pilgrims, came to these shores, they instituted here the customs that they had followed in the old country. They were religious people and Sunday was their holy day, on which they refrained from doing work or conducting business. They came to America to flee persecution against members of their faith, and hoped to establish in this land a society in which they could practice their beliefs and customs freely and without harassment. They established their custom as secular law in the colonies, and later it became the law of many states: Sunday was the Sabbath and the prohibition of work was prescribed for that day.

The laws enacted in many states prohibited members of all faiths from engaging in business on Sunday. Even Jews, who kept Saturday as their Sabbath, were forced to remain closed on Sunday as well. This imposed great hardships on many *shomer Shabbos* businesses. To have to close for two consecutive days was almost impossible for many businessmen.

In addition to forbidding business transactions, many other activities were also banned by these laws, such as sports and entertainment. The laws came to be called "blue laws," after the blue paper on which such laws were printed in seventeenth-century New Haven.

Since we live in a secular society, many aspects of these laws have been repealed over the years. The restrictions on entertainment and sports events have been relaxed. Even while it was still the law for businesses to remain closed on Sundays, this law was often not strictly enforced. Many *shomrei Shabbos* did open their stores on Sundays, and the police didn't enforce the blue laws. The Orthodox Jews needed the income they made on that day to stay in business.

However, at one point during the 1940's, it seems that some business owners began to complain. They felt that the religious Jews had an advantage in being allowed to remain open on Sundays while they were closed, even though the reverse was true on Saturdays: Their stores were open while the Orthodox-owned businesses were closed. The complaints reached high authorities and a blitz against the Orthodox Jews was launched. Anyone who did business on Sunday began to receive tickets for doing so, and people were summoned to court for violating the law. With this harsh punishment, many Jewish business owners found it almost impossible to remain in business.

Rabbi Chaim Uri Lipschitz, the famous author and lecturer, told me of the following incident in which he was a participant. Four Jews — Rabbi Kalmanowitz of Mir, who was one of those instrumental in rescuing the entire Mirrer Yeshiva from beneath the boots of the Nazis; Reb Chaim; Rabbi Chaim Uri Lipschitz, and Rabbi Simcha Weissman — went before the judge of the State Supreme Court. As they entered the judge's chambers, Reb Chaim started to dance and sing, "*Shabbos Kodesh, Shabbos Kodesh.*" He was praying, dancing, and singing fervently the words, "Holy Shabbos, holy Shabbos," trying to impress upon the judge the importance of their message. Conversely, next to Reb Chaim stood Rabbi Kalmanowitz, who was crying bitterly, "*Shabbos Kodesh, Shabbos Kodesh.*" Two polar opposites, but with one goal, *Shabbos Kodesh*. It was a rare moment indeed. The judge was impressed by their sincerity, and promised that he would do all he could for them.

The police subsequently halted their drive of ticketing Shabbos observers for being open on Sunday; today, in New York, it is perfectly legal to conduct business on Sunday.

A Narrow Escape

ONE DAY, REB CHAIM WAS WALKING through the deserted streets of Williamsburg. Suddenly, he saw a group of young toughs approaching him in the distance. Their eyes were directed toward him, spying an easy mark. To them, an old Jew with a beard, who probably didn't even speak English, was easy prey. It wasn't immediately clear whether they were about to rob him or "merely" to have a good time taunting him — a favored pastime of anti-Semites for generations. As they sidled up to him, ready to start their ugly game, Reb Chaim beat them to the punch. He opened his mouth and said to them, "Good morning, boys. It is always a pleasure to see such fine young American youths."

The boys were thunderstruck. He spoke English better than they did! And he had called them fine American boys! The wind was taken out of their sails, and they continued on their way.

A Miracle?

WE CONSTANTLY HEAR ABOUT RACIAL and anti-Semitic deeds and remarks. Violent acts and graffiti expressing hatred toward the Jews are found in many places. Synagogues have been defaced with swastikas and epithets of animosity and hatred towards our people. In Reb Chaim's day, however, this disease was even stronger and more virulent.

In his youth, about seventy years ago, Reb Chaim was walking peacefully on the Lower East Side of New York when he was suddenly surrounded by a gang of hoodlums who began to taunt him, casting aspersions against his religion. They grabbed him and threw him down into a cellar, slamming the metal doors behind him and locking him in. The doors were of heavy metal with handles only on the outside. It took a fairly strong man to open these doors using the outside handles; from the inside, it was nearly impossible to open them, so when one descended into the cellar, it was imperative that he leave the doors open.

Reb Chaim was frightened and bewildered by his predicament.

How could he possibly escape? He didn't lose his head, though, and turned to his only refuge in times of trouble, to *Hashem*. He raised his hands to *Hashem*, crying out the words of *Shema Yisrael*. In raising his hands in supplication he grazed the doors, which then sprang open with hardly any effort! He jumped out of the cellar and rapidly ran for home. Later, when recalling this incident, he was convinced that Elijah the prophet or another angel had come to his rescue as an answer to his prayers.

Saved by His Tzitzis

THE FOLLOWING INCIDENT INVOLVING REB CHAIM is so well known that it has become part of our folklore. Yeshiva students have repeated it with wonder and amazement. The uniqueness of this occurrence is another factor that has made it so much a part of the public domain.

Every morning Reb Chaim would rise early to start his long day of fulfilling his charitable and religious obligations. He never knew what he would be required to do or who would call upon him for help. He had to be ready at all times, and he was. First of all, he would immerse himself in the *mikveh* to prepare himself for prayer.

On this particular day, it was still dark out as Reb Chaim left his home. Times then were more peaceful and crime-free than they are today, and Reb Chaim was never afraid. However, on this day, as Reb Chaim was walking through the nearly deserted streets of Williamsburg, thinking of the charitable acts he would perform that day, he was suddenly accosted by a hulking male figure. Without warning he approached Reb Chaim, ready to pounce on him.

Reb Chaim always wore his *tzitzis* out, and at that particular moment he was unconsciously holding them between his fingers. Startled by this sudden advance, he raised his hands, with the *tzitzis* wrapped around them, and pointed them at his attacker. The man took one quick look and shouted, "Don't shoot! Don't shoot!" Apparently, in the dark, he mistook the pointed fingers

Chapter Eleven: Midos — Character / 153

with the *tzitzis* as some sort of weapon, and began to run away from the perplexed Reb Chaim as fast as he could.

Catching a Thief

IN THE PRIME OF REB CHAIM'S LIFE, Williamsburg was a very quiet, serene area, relatively free from crime. The streets were safe at all hours of the day or night. However, at one time one of Reb Chaim's neighbors was plagued by petty thievery.

Near Reb Chaim's home was a small *shomer Shabbos* grocery which had been robbed several times. The robberies had all taken place at night, after the store had closed. The store was not large and the owner made but a small *parnassah* from it; he could ill afford to absorb the losses resulting from the break-ins that had hit his store. The police were unable to stop this rash of crime, and the owner was afraid that if the robberies continued, he would be forced to close his store. The robberies were draining his income to the extent that he could barely afford to remain open.

No solution seemed forthcoming to this problem. The robberies continued. One night, during the holiday of *Succos*, Reb Chaim was sitting in his *succah* partaking of his meal when his daughter Shirley called out to him that she spotted a man running across the roof. Reb Chaim jumped up, quickly armed himself with a baseball bat, and waited alertly in the dark. He soon noticed someone jumping down from his neighbor's roof into the yard next door, where the grocery store was located. Reb Chaim bravely leaped over the fence separating his property from that of the grocery, and confronted the robber with his bat. He kept the thief cornered until the police arrived to apprehend him.

The mystery was solved, the burglaries ceased, and the storekeeper was able to resume normal operations without any additional fear of theft.

Reb Chaim was ready to help a fellow Jew in all situations. His charity was not limited to financial assistance; he also offered physical help when necessary.

OUR RABBIS TEACH US that if one saves a person's life it is considered as though he has saved an entire world. This is the

Saving a Life

value that the Torah places on human life. Most people, however, never get the chance to perform such an outstanding deed. And most of us do not know how we would react if the opportunity did present itself, especially if the possibility of bodily harm or danger were present.

In the corner house on Division Avenue and Wilson lived a widow named Mrs. Posner, who had the difficult task of raising three children by herself. She was a young and pious woman, who devoted what little free time she had to collecting money for Ezras Torah, a fund for needy Torah scholars.

One day Mrs. Posner decided to wash the outside of her windows. She positioned a chair on the shanty roof outside her window and stood on it. Suddenly the chair slipped or she lost her balance, and with an ear-splitting shriek, she began to fall.

At that moment Reb Chaim happened to be walking in the direction from which the shrieks were coming. He instantly realized what had happened and, with a G-d-given burst of speed and strength, managed to race to the spot beneath Mrs. Posner's window, open his arms wide and break her fall. An ambulance was summoned and Mrs. Posner, hurt but alive, was taken to the hospital, where she remained for several weeks.

Mrs. Posner lived to a ripe old age and, interestingly, was a resident in Aishel Avraham at the same time Reb Chaim lived there.

EVEN TODAY, SEVERAL YEARS AFTER REB CHAIM'S PASSING, his name evokes magical responses. Mention his name, and doors that

Reb Chaim's Reputation: As Good as Cash

were previously closed will open; cold, reserved people suddenly become transformed into different human beings. Emotions wax strong and feelings run high. Just say, "Do you remember Chaim Gelb?" and people will respond, "Of course! He always approached me for charity, and I always gave him as much as I could." People express the feeling of pride that they were his associates in this tremendous *mitzvah*. They were honored by his asking them to participate in the *mitzvah* with him, and remember him with a strong feeling of nostalgia.

"Reb Chaim Gelb? He was a *tzaddik*," people respond when his name is mentioned. "He was a giant!"

"He cheered us up when he entered our *shul*," say others.

"I remember him from my yeshiva days — he gave me a knish so I could make a *brachah*," recalls a middle-aged man.

"He wouldn't take more than a nickel from me, because I was a young *yeshiva bachur* and he felt that I couldn't afford more," reminisces another.

A recent episode is yet another manifestation of the warm feelings that the broad Orthodox masses had for Reb Chaim Gelb. One summer not long ago, one of his grandchildren, who was spending the summer in the mountains with his family, was shopping in a food store there. After selecting his groceries, he realized that he did not have enough cash with him to cover the full bill. He approached the proprietor and asked whether it would be all right for him to pay half in cash and the rest by check.

The proprietor refused this request, stating that since his was a summer business, he did not know the customers well and it was his policy not to accept checks. People came to the mountains from all over, and he did not wish to follow them back to their year-round homes trying to collect his bills; thus he maintained a strict cash-only business.

The young man was faced with the dilemma of having to return home without the needed groceries. He pleaded, "Look, I work at this bungalow colony and everyone there knows me. You can ask anyone about me, and they will all vouch for me that I am a *ben Torah* and completely honest." But the storekeeper could not be moved. "Cash only," he reiterated. He did not wish to take any chances with his small business, since he could not afford any unnecessary losses.

The young man was also undaunted. Again he appealed to the grocer, "My father is a well-known rabbi in Brooklyn, and he is highly respected. Do you think I would do anything to besmirch his name?" The grocer replied that he had never heard of the man's father, and he would not change his policy.

Time was running out; it was almost closing hour. The customer made one last desperate plea. "All right. You don't know me, and you don't know my father. But perhaps I can give you another guarantee which may make you change your mind."

"My mind is made up. Nothing will change it."

"What if I were to tell you that I am Reb Chaim Gelb's grandson?"

The grocer looked up in amazement. Without another word, he stretched out his hand to accept the young man's check. The name of Reb Chaim had evoked such strong memories and respect that the storekeeper could no longer refuse the request of Reb Chaim's grandson. Reb Chaim was a blessing to his people during his lifetime, and continued to be so even after his passing.

A Fond Recollection

DEAR RABBI FISHER,

IN THE YEARS THAT I LIVED ACROSS THE WAY from Chaim Gelb on Division Avenue, between Wilson and Ross Streets, everyone in the religious community knew one another. All knew that R' Chaim devoted his life to his religion.

My husband, Rabbi Yerachmiel (Roy) Chavkin, was the *gabbai* in Mesivta Torah Vodaath during the summer. Every week Chaim Gelb would bring him a sizable contribution for Torah Vodaath from his collections.

When Chaim Gelb *davened* before the *amud* on Friday night in Yeshiva Torah Vodaath, his beautiful voice was inspiring to all those present. During the weekday morning services he would encourage the students of the *yeshiva ketanah* to come in and answer *Amen*.

Even after forty years, my husband clearly remembers the fervor with which R' Chaim answered "*Amen*." When he prayed, he used his entire body, and would bend very low during *Shemoneh Esrai*.

In those days it was a problem to get young people to continue in yeshiva beyond elementary school. Chaim Gelb went out with great enthusiasm and encouraged them by being a living example, exhibiting his religious fervor to everyone around him. In those days you did not generally see such open and fervent expression of religious ideals as he showed.

Was there ever a businessman who devoted so much of his time to supporting institutions as the one and only Chaim Gelb did?

No one knows how many institutions depended upon him. He was a man of tremendous foresight and was ahead of his time. You have to understand the state of religion in America in those days to fully appreciate his deeds. In those days there were few yeshivos and only one or two *mesivta* high schools in the entire country.

Rabbi Aharon Kotler was able to borrow large sums of money regularly from the bank to support his Lakewood Yeshiva on the basis of Chaim Gelb's signature.

People who would normally give a collector a small coin would give Chaim Gelb large amounts because they had so much confidence in him. He had extraordinary self-restraint, and was able to withstand criticism by people who thought he was too open about his religious devotion. He had a reputation for integrity that was beyond reproach. Who knows how many people were influenced by him to be more open about their religion? His enthusiasm was contagious.

His name was used in conversations to represent someone who was overly exuberant about his religion. People would say, "What are you becoming, a Chaim Gelb man?" Though I considered this a compliment, people who were shy about their religious expression meant it as a criticism.

Though my husband has taught in prominent yeshivos for over forty years and is well acquainted with famous *rebbeim*, whenever he imagines what a fully devoted Jew would be, he pictures Chaim Gelb.

Sincerely,
Mrs. Libby Gross Chavkin

CHAPTER TWELVE
Reb Chaim's Words of Wisdom

REB CHAIM BELIEVED THAT A JEW should follow a good, healthy diet and eat well to maintain his strength, so he would have the physical ability to perform *mitzvos*. He would emphasize this concept with the expression, *"Men darf zein a Eat (Yid)."* To be a good, functioning Jew, one must eat well.

❈ ❈ ❈

Reb Chaim pointed out a very important concept in Judaism in the following fashion, utilizing a passage from the Torah: *"V'atem hadveikim baHashem Elokeichem chayim kulchem hayom."*

V'atem: What is the Jew's "atom" power that gives us strength?
Hadveikim baHashem: When we cling to G-d.

Putting it simply: What is a Jew's atom power? How do we acquire it? By cleaving to G-d. Our power is derived from the spirituality of our people.

❈ ❈ ❈

Reb Chaim expressed deep insight into how we should educate our children and teach them *Yiddishkeit*. He was wont to use the following analogy to teach his concept of *chinuch*:

If one heats an object with a flame or another hot object, the article that is being warmed up will never become as hot as the flame from which it gets its warmth. It will get warm, for certain, but rarely will the object get as warm as the one from which it gets its heat. So Reb Chaim deduced: If parents are zealous and burning with their commitment to *Yiddishkeit*, their offspring will at the very least be warm and devoted to Torah. On the other hand, if the parents are only lukewarm in their adherence to *Yiddishkeit*, then the offspring may have a cool attitude to Torah or, even worse, may be cold and totally disenchanted.

Our commitment will be reflected in our children. The stronger our observance and the examples and patterns we set for our children, the stronger and warmer will be their observance of Torah.

❈ ❈ ❈

Reb Chaim was always irked by a common expression which we all use. Whenever he heard it, he could not refrain from criticizing the one who had made such a seemingly innocuous statement.

We have often heard the question, "Does he make a living?" Reb Chaim would retort to this, "*Make* a living? What kind of talk is that? No one *makes* a living — *Hashem gives* it! We ourselves make nothing!" He rejected this phrase because it inferred that we make life; however, only *Hashem* can make life.

"One should ask, 'How is his *parnassah*?' rather than, 'Does he make a living?' " Reb Chaim would declare. "It is not proper for a Jew to talk in this manner." Reb Chaim was aware of G-d's presence at all times and in everything, and careful to fulfill his duty to Him.

❈ ❈ ❈

Reb Chaim found the flame of Judaism in a piece of fruit. Once, while eating a plum, Reb Chaim turned to me and said, "Look at this — it teaches us *Yiddishkeit*. In Yiddish a plum is called a *flaum*, which also means flame. Inside there is a pit, called in Yiddish a *kehr*, which also means to turn. So, it points out that a Jew must possess a warm, burning flame of Torah, constantly *kehren* — "turning" — toward *Hashem*."

Although in this generation our people do not have men or scholars of the stature of the Vilna *Gaon* or the *Chofetz Chaim*, Reb Chaim pointed out that we as a people can attain their greatness collectively.

That is, if everyone would join in and participate in the performance of a *mitzvah* with the correct *kavanah*, zeal and spirit, we could be just as effective as the previously mentioned *gedolim*. In other words, collectively, as a people, we can be the equivalent of the Vilna *Gaon* or the *Chofetz Chaim*.

✻ ✻ ✻

Every word that a person utters is not to be looked at lightly, according to Reb Chaim, but has to be examined and treated in a sincere manner. A good example is the following experience which I had when I was first married. I remarked to Reb Chaim nonchalantly, "I am going down to the store to buy something."

Reb Chaim quickly rebuked me and said, "A Jew never goes down; he always goes up." In this simple conversation he was reminding me of a profound concept that should be in one's thoughts at all times: A Jew must always go up; spiritually, we must always continue to grow. The conversation had been simple and superficial, but to Reb Chaim, whose thoughts and being were wrapped up in G-dliness, every word could be utilized in a holy context in reference to one's existence as a Jew. This was but another indication of his constant awareness of Torah and *Yiddishkeit* and its applicability to our everyday language and life.

✻ ✻ ✻

Reb Chaim by nature liked people. He always was happy and cheerful. Concerning his nature we can say, "*Lev tov mishteh tamid* — He who has a good heart is always in the position of one enjoying a good meal." Reb Chaim's heart was full of love for every fellow Jew; he was friendly and cheerful to whoever he encountered. He would cite a homiletic interpretation of a phrase in *parshas Vayetzei*: When Yaakov *Avinu* met the shepherds at the well where he was to meet Rachel for the first time, he told them, *"Hashku hatzon ulechu re'u* — Water the flock and graze them." Reb Chaim interpreted *"Hashku hatzon* — water the flock," as referring to making a *"L'chaim"* with one's fellow Jews. *"Lechu re'u"* means "Go out and be friendly," as *"re'u"* has the same root as the Hebrew word meaning friendship. He took the meaning of this Biblical phrase to be that one should always be open and friendly towards one's fellow Jew.

❦ ❦ ❦

When people greeted Reb Chaim by name, he would invariably reply with his homespun remark, *"Zoll dir Chaim in dem kop* — May *Hashem* bestow life upon your head." Although the greeter was merely mentioning his name, Chaim, he inferred that the speaker wished to give him *chaim*, life — so he returned the blessing with fervor. Thus was the greatness of his love for his fellow Jew.

❦ ❦ ❦

The following was related to me by Rabbi Nosson Hirshberg, at the time I met him a *maggid shiur* at Yeshiva Mercaz HaTorah of Belle Harbor.

During the month of *Elul*, while collecting *tzedakah*, Reb Chaim would make a strange request of his donors. He asked for pennies. When people looked at him quizzically he would explain, "Pennies are made of copper, and the Hebrew word כַּפֶּר means atonement. What more propitious moment could one seek atonement if not during *Elul*, the month that precedes *Rosh Hashanah*. Our copper for *tzedakah* will cause *Hashem* to reciprocate and *'copper'* our sins and bestow a good year upon us."

CHAPTER THIRTEEN
Reb Chaim's Final Years

IN 1979, WHEN REB CHAIM WAS eighty-six years old, Aishel Avraham opened in Williamsburg. This was a home for the aged, run under Orthodox auspices, and its primary function was to serve those Orthodox Jews who had special needs as required by our religion. Unfortunately, by that time Reb Chaim was no longer physically able to continue his exhausting rounds and to pursue the life style to which he had become accustomed. His feet were no longer able to take him to the synagogues, wedding halls, hospitals, and all the other places he visited to collect *tzedakah* and help the needy. His lifetime avocation of collecting charity and providing succor to the indigent could no longer be pursued.

Being fiercely independent, Reb Chaim did not wish to become a burden to his children, and he adamantly refused to move in with any of them. He decided that the wisest course for him would be to enter Aishel Avraham and to spend the remaining days of his life in serenity there. He was officially the first entrant to that institution. Aishel Avraham was equipped to supply all the religious needs of the residents. There was a synagogue on the premises, where the residents could *daven* three times daily, and the kitchen was strictly *glatt* kosher. The Home was located in the very neighborhood in which Reb Chaim had spent most of his adult life, among the people he loved so dearly. Many of his old acquaintances came to visit him frequently. The people who ran Aishel Avraham treated him royally, with great respect. Even the members of the staff, most of whom were not Jewish, went out of their way to make him comfortable and happy. They recognized that this man was a *tzaddik*, and that he enjoyed being there.

Reb Chaim had his own private room and bath in Aishel Avraham. When one entered his room, one could immediately discern by its character that this was Reb Chaim's room: signs about Shabbos observance covered the walls. Upon seeing him and meeting his gaze, one could sense that here was an unusual person. An aura of peace and serenity emanated from his face, and one could recognize him as being *same'ach bechelko*, satisfied with his portion in life. Old age doesn't automatically bring about this state, as I was able to observe. Many old people are depressed, bitter and melancholy. The nurses advised visitors many times to avoid making friendly overtures towards certain residents who were apt to react negatively and even become abusive. Reb Chaim's face, though, was illuminated with *kedushah*, as it is written, "The wisdom of man lights up his face." His mind was flooded with the memories of all the magnificent deeds he had been instrumental in accomplishing throughout his long life. In his old age he was reaping the harvest of his productive years.

As mentioned earlier, the staff at Aishel Avraham treated him with the utmost respect. However, he reciprocated their courtesy, for whenever he was served he never failed to offer thanks to the person performing the service for him. Although these were paid employees simply doing their jobs, he made them feel as if they were performing *chessed*, kindness, not simply fulfilling their duties.

Many people came to visit him. Old acquaintances or people he had met through his work were among the many who thronged to see him. People who came to visit other residents of the home always made a stop to greet Reb Chaim once they became aware that he was there as well.

Individuals who had contributed to his charity fund over the years brought money to him at Aishel Avraham. They felt honored to be able to continue this practice. Although Reb Chaim

*Reb Chaim's 87th birthday at Aishel Avraham
with children, grandchildren and great-grandchildren*

was not personally able to distribute the funds he received, he still made sure that the needy would not be deprived of his help.

The first year of his residence passed uneventfully. At the end of this year, the family decided to convene to celebrate Reb Chaim's eighty-seventh birthday. Although during his lifetime he never did celebrate his birthday, we all felt that it would be proper to do so now. The facilities of Aishel Avraham were opened to us, and there was ample space for a fine celebration. The refreshments were purchased and prepared by various family members, and the entire clan gathered together on a Sunday. Many were musically inclined, and the singing was loud and joyous.

Reb Chaim was seated on a chair in the middle of the room, and the family gathered around him — children, grandchildren, and great-grandchildren. We sang all the songs that he loved and that he himself had sung and taught us when he was well and active. When our voices rose in a strong crescendo with the words, *"Moshe emes v'Soraso emes,"* tears streamed down his cheeks. To Reb Chaim, this scene was reminiscent of the one in the Torah

Chapter Thirteen: Final Years / 165

when Yaakov *Avinu's* twelve sons gathered around him to say the *Shema* and proclaim G-d's unity. The words "Moshe is true and his Torah is true" stirred his innermost feelings, and he shed tears of joy and *nachas*.

Reb Chaim was a very strong and contained man, and other than at his wife's funeral, I had never seen him shed a tear. However at that moment, when his entire family showed their loyalty and devotion to him by singing the words according to which he had lived his life, he was utterly moved. He had the *zechus*, the merit, to see his traditions and beliefs being carried on by his many offspring. That one moment epitomized the culmination and fruition of his life's work. At that moment we all realized how right we had been to organize this birthday celebration. G-d wanted Reb Chaim to have this rare moment of total joy, and in his remaining years we made it a tradition to celebrate Reb Chaim's birthday in the same fashion.

Two tragic events marred Reb Chaim's stay at Aishel Avraham. First, his only son, Avigdor, passed away, leaving three children. After consulting with several *rabbanim* about his condition, the decision was made not to inform Reb Chaim of this tragedy because of his frail and weakened condition.

Although we did not tell him about it, we had the distinct feeling that he was aware of the tragedy. He obviously missed the visits of his son and must have realized what had transpired. However, he also knew that we did not want to worry him, and he thus played along and did not upset us with his intuitive knowledge; this was the greatness of the man.

When his beloved daughter Rose passed away three weeks before Reb Chaim himself did, he was already in a coma, and thus never knew about it.

In his ninety-first year Reb Chaim was seized by a severe stroke from which he never fully recovered. After his stay in the hospital he was returned to Aishel Avraham, but unfortunately he had been deprived of a great deal of physical movement.

He was stricken later by yet another stroke and was again rushed to the hospital. At least one family member remained with

The Gelb twins, Chaim and Shimon Yiddle at age 87.

him at all times; a yeshiva *bachur* was engaged to help in this 24-hour-a-day vigil. Reb Chaim's throat muscles had been paralyzed, and he had to be fed intravenously.

The noted Talmudic commentator, the Maharsha, comments on the episode in the Talmud which relates the suffering that the great tannaitic scholar, Rebbi, endured. He notes that the reason that one finds so many Torah greats inflicted with stomach problems is that man consists of both body and spirit. The spirit can never attain its loftiest possible heights when attached to a body which subsists on material objects. *Hashem*, wishing to purify these great individuals, deprives them of the ability to enjoy food, the material object. In this manner, too, man becomes more like the angels, reaching new heights. So it was in the case of Reb Chaim: His stroke had deprived him of the ability to eat. He lived

Chapter Thirteen: Final Years / 167

by the spirit alone. He lived all his ninety-one years as a *tzaddik*, and passed away as one.

The funeral was held in Williamsburg. Reb Chaim had spent almost all his life there, and it was only fitting that his final moments on earth should be spent there. He was eulogized by many prominent *rabbanim* and by members of his family, and eulogies appeared in newspapers both in this country and in Israel. Even *Olomeinu* [a popular children's magazine] ran an article about him so that children in schools across the country could learn about his remarkable life and emulate him.

One year later, on his *yahrzeit*, Aishel Avraham made a *seudah* in his memory. At this luncheon his deeds were recounted so they might never be forgotten. This book is the result.